Wellpreneur

The Ultimate Guide for Wellness
Entrepreneurs to Nail Your Niche
and Find Clients Online

Wellpreneur

The Ultimate Guide for Wellness Entrepreneurs to Nail Your Niche and Find Clients Online

Amanda Cook

YACUM HILL
PRESS

WellpreneurBook.com
For print or media interviews with Amanda please contact
info@wellpreneuronline.com

ISBN: 978-0-9957443-1-8

Author Photo: J. Nichole Sears
Cover Design: Vanessa Maynard
Book Design: Gillian Katsoulis
Book Editing: Laura Hanly

Wellpreneur (n):

1. An entrepreneur in the field of health and wellness.

2. An entrepreneur who considers and prioritizes personal and communal wellbeing while building a business.

Table of Contents

Introduction

"Instead of wondering when your next vacation is, maybe you ought to set up a life you don't need to escape from."

— Seth Godin, *Tribes*

Welcome, Wellpreneur.

When I graduated from my health coach training program in 2012, I felt both energized and anxious. I was convinced health coaching was my path to leave my corporate job for a life of freedom and abundance. But I was anxious because I didn't want to be a health coach in the traditional sense. I wanted to work *online*. And I had no idea what that would look like or how to get there.

At that time, just a few years ago, the traditional advice when starting a wellness business was to hold workshops and book in free consultations with potential clients. But how could that work online? I wanted to see examples of wellpreneurs creating thriving businesses online... But where were they? It was nearly impossible to find real people doing what I wanted to do.

My search for successful online wellpreneurs inspired me to start The Wellpreneur Podcast. Over the past three years, I've interviewed more than 112 successful wellness entrepreneurs and experts about how to grow a wellness business online. They've shared stories of success and struggle, advice and lessons about marketing, business, productivity and wellbeing. These successful wellpreneurs are health coaches, acupuncturists, natural beauty brands, personal chefs, personal trainers, yoga teachers, healthy media companies, restaurateurs and more.

I noticed two major trends with these interviews:

1) You can use online marketing to grow *every* kind of wellness business. It all comes down to your creativity and vision.

2) Every successful online wellness business has a system to bring more of the right people to their website, and to turn them into paying clients.

As the podcast grew, I had the chance to speak with hundreds of wellpreneurs at all levels of business. When I spoke with wellpreneurs who were struggling to get traction online, they were always missing the second part: the system. They spent hours fixing their websites or "engaging" on social media. They tried running webinars, or automating social media updates, or blogging more frequently, but they still weren't getting any clients! What quickly became clear is that **the key difference between successful and struggling online wellpreneurs is that the successful wellpreneurs had a system to find new clients online.** Rather than trying every new online marketing hack, successful wellpreneurs put in place a simple system to consistently bring the right people to their website, and turn them into paying clients.

At the time, I was already working closely with wellpreneurs on technology, websites, tools and automation. But observing how my successful podcast guests were growing their businesses made me change my approach. Instead of focusing on tools, I shifted to helping my clients create a simple system. It would be slightly different for each client depending on their brand, strengths and interests, but the primary building blocks were the same. There was always a clear path to convert a website visitor into a paying client. The tools were secondary.

Suddenly, online business felt a lot easier to explain. You don't need to evaluate every new tool, instead, you need to set up your system first. Then it becomes clear where you need to focus your time, energy and money.

That's the Organic Growth System, and it's what you're going to learn in this book.

No matter your stage of business, you can use the simplicity and power of this system to find clients online. If you're just starting out (even if you're still in training!) you can put the pieces in place to build your audience and start getting client inquiries. If you have an established business, you can use this system to improve your lead generation, or even add a steady new stream of client inquiries to your business. This system works for solopreneurs as well as brands. And you don't have to be a technical genius to make it work for you.

Who Is This Book For?

This book is for you if you're a wellness entrepreneur who is new to online marketing, or if you're not happy with the results you're getting from your current online marketing.

If you're not getting a steady stream of new client inquiries online, if you ever feel overwhelmed with online marketing, or if you're not sure where to focus to make your online marketing effective, this book will help.

While many of my examples are tailored to solopreneurs (individual wellness entrepreneurs), the system we discuss can be applied to almost any wellness business, whether you have a physical location (like a clinic or gym), sell physical products, or see clients in-person as well as online.

In my system, the *marketing* is done online, but the delivery of the product or service doesn't have to be! For example:

- You could have an in-person business working in your local area, and still use online marketing to attract new customers and deepen your relationship with existing customers.

- You could sell physical products from a physical location like a shop, or via eCommerce online.

- You could run a hybrid business where you deliver both online and offline products and services. For example, a personal trainer might train clients in person, but also offer online personal training sessions and pre-recorded workouts for clients who are travelling.

- You could work completely online, delivering digital information products and virtual services (like coaching) to clients around the world.

(And there are numerous other combinations of online and offline to fit your dreams, goals and work preferences too. The possibilities are endless!)

None of these options is better than another. It really comes down to what kind of business you want to create, how you like to work with clients and your vision for your life and your business.

There is so much potential and flexibility with online wellness businesses specifically because everyone's journey into wellness is different.

Just think about the dramatically different tribes of people who comprise the wellness industry:

- Raw vegans

- Paleo CrossFit junkies

- Yogis who sip organic cold-pressed green juices in their designer yoga gear

- And many more!

Each of these groups has found their own path to wellness. You might fit in one of these groups (or none of them), but I guarantee you don't fit in all of them. And that's OK. It's the same with your potential customers.

Because the journey into wellness is such an individual one, there's plenty of room for different brands, products and practitioners to meet the needs of consumers. With an online business, you don't *need* to create a product or service that goes mass-market. You can help the people who have the exact challenges you're most passionate about and help them in a way that lights you up — because you can find each other online.

And don't worry: using the system in this book as a framework, you'll be able to make your online marketing feel authentically *you*. You'll see that effective online marketing doesn't need to be scammy and salesy, or overly glossy, polished, perfect and intimidating (yes, Instagram, I'm thinking about you!). You can bring your own unique personality to online marketing to attract ideal clients who resonate with YOU and your style.

How to Use This Book

In this book, you'll learn my entire five-step Organic Growth System to find your ideal customers online, bring them to your website, and turn them into paying customers.

It's the same system I use in my business, as well as with my private coaching and consulting clients. It's also what I teach in my online course, Wellpreneur Marketing Bootcamp.

Once you know this simple system to turn website visitors into paying clients, you'll never look at online marketing the same again. It's also effective for eliminating overwhelm and helping you focus on exactly what you need to do to improve your results.

I recommend you read through this entire book first, to make sure you understand the big picture of the system and how it can work for you and your business.

Then go back and start from the beginning to implement it. I know it can be tempting to skip ahead (especially the initial vision and target market chapters), but please don't do this. These steps are absolutely critical to your success with online marketing, so if you're going to take the time to set up systems in your business, do it the right way from the beginning.

Throughout the book you'll also read excerpts from my interviews with successful wellness entrepreneurs to inspire you and provide real-world examples of how to grow your business online.

And because we're talking about online marketing, remember that the landscape changes quickly. I've created a Book Bonuses section on my website which I'll keep up to date with my latest tech recommendations, worksheets and checklists to take action on what you're learning, and the complete audio interviews with the wellpreneurs featured in the book. You'll also get access to our Wellpreneur Community Facebook Group so you can connect with other wellpreneurs around the world.

Go to: WellpreneurBook.com/bonus to access the Book Bonuses

The book is organized into 11 chapters:

Chapters 1, 2, 3 and 4 help you define your vision, your customer, and your offerings. You'll define your WHY, WHO, WHAT and HOW, key components of any marketing strategy. These chapters are absolutely critical to your success online and I urge you to complete all of the exercises even if you feel you've done this before or if you're already selling online. *Please don't start implementing the rest of the system until you have completed these.*

Chapter 5 is an explanation of my Organic Growth System to turn website visitors into paying clients. This is the big picture overview that has generated "aha!" moments for so many wellpreneurs, and will change your perspective of online marketing forever.

Chapters 6 through 10 dive deep into each step of the Organic Growth System, so you know exactly how to implement it in your own business.

And finally, Chapter 11 shares my favorite tips, advice and strategies for easily incorporating online marketing into your business. I've included this because all the thinking in the world won't bring you customers online — you have to put it into action!

 Throughout the book you'll see this symbol, which indicates a step where wellpreneurs often get stuck or spend too long in indecision. I'll give you some tips to make sure you keep moving forward without getting stuck here too!

By the end of this book you'll know exactly where to find your ideal clients online and how to turn them into paying clients. You'll have clarity and focus around your online marketing. You'll feel confident about how to build your business, so you can focus on what you really love to do — spreading health and wellness!

Chapter 1

Your Big Vision

"Would you tell me, please, which way I ought to go from here?"

"That depends a good deal on where you want to get to," said the Cat.

"I don't much care where —" said Alice.

"Then it doesn't matter which way you go," said the Cat.

"—so long as I get SOMEWHERE," Alice added as an explanation.

"Oh, you're sure to do that," said the Cat, "if you only walk long enough."

— Lewis Carroll, *Alice in Wonderland*

"The secret to every success, lies not in what or even who you know, but in clearly 'seeing' where you want to go. And going."

— The Universe, *Notes From the Universe*

When you imagine your ideal wellness business, what comes to mind?

- A bustling wellness center with plush furnishings and a team of expert practitioners?

- A sweet café and yoga space in a historic building?

- Working in an established clinic as a solo practitioner?

- Running a company which hosts wellness retreats around the world?

- Launching a new healthy food product?

- Working solely online running detox programs and individual coaching.

...or something else entirely?

If you're like many wellpreneurs I meet, you don't really know where you want to end up — as long as it's not where you are right now!

If that sounds like you, make sure heed the advice from the Cheshire Cat. You're sure to end up somewhere, if you just walk long enough... but it may not be where you wanted to go.

I believe it's possible to create any type of wellness business that you want... But first you have to decide what you want.

The funny thing is, for many wellpreneurs, this process isn't as easy as it sounds.

You would think that the idea of dreaming up an ideal business would be fun, exciting, motivating and expansive. But for many wellpreneurs it creates waves of fear about choosing the wrong thing, missing out on something better, or even fear of not achieving a big goal, so they keep their business vision small or nonexistent!

So while you might be itching to start blogging, dream up ways to get published in The Huffington Post, or create a world-changing online program, let's take a little time upfront to get clear on where you're going.

I know it FEELS like this dreaming and scheming is slowing you down, but what will really slow you down is spending…

- Weeks writing blog posts and building an email sequence, and then realizing you don't have any idea how to generate revenue.

- Months developing what you think is the"perfect" online course, only to find that no one will buy it.

- Money on a big social media promotion, without a system in place to handle the leads that come in.

While you don't need a complete business plan to start your business, you DO need to understand where you're going, who you serve, and how you're going to generate revenue.

(Yes, revenue. You're a business owner, and that means you have to take ownership of your money — or lack of it. Money and revenue are not dirty words, and if you don't have a clear plan for generating revenue then you'll likely have a hobby blog about wellness. And that's perfectly OK if that's what you want to do — but in that case, better keep your day job!)

So, what do you want to create? What does your ideal life and business look like?

It's such a simple question. But the answer is not always that straightforward.

Amanda Cook

It's often a lot easier to work out what we DON'T want. Maybe you *don't* want to be stuck in a corporate job, or *don't* want to be working long hours for little money, or *don't* want to work for a company that feels ethically incompatible with your beliefs, or *don't* want to have a strict time schedule to your day.

But it's a lot more motivating to work towards a goal than away from something you don't like. For example, there are lots of ways to not have a corporate job, but not all of them will make you happy. Instead of running away from what we don't want, let's start envisioning a life and business that will really light you up.

Exercise: Your Ideal Business and Life

I want you to spend a little time *feeling* what you want for your business and life.

Close your eyes and imagine a day in your life, when you have your ultimate business.

See yourself waking up.

- *Where are you? Where do you live?*

- *Who is with you? What's your morning routine like?*

- *Do you go to work? Where?*

- *Are you alone or with others? What kind of tasks do you do during the day?*

- *What kind of clients or customers do you work with?*

- *What do you do in the afternoon? What about the evening?*

- *What are the most exciting things happening in your life and business that week, month or year?*

- *How do you feel about your life and business?*

- *What are you looking forward to in the future?*

You might not know all the specific details, but you'll uncover the *feelings* you want to create in your life and the type of business you want to create.

You might be surprised at what comes up.

Now, get a pen and paper for a free-writing exercise. Make two columns (or two sheets) — "Life" and "Business."

(When I say to "free-write", I mean for you to silence the critical voice in your head that whispers *"you can't do that!"*, *"that's impossible"*, *"how are you going to do that?"* Don't worry about those doubts. This is the time to get it all out on paper, not to figure out how you're going to do it. That comes later! For now, just write everything down.)

Set the timer for 10 minutes, and just allow your creativity and dreams to flow as you write about your ideal life. What would you like to create in your life and business? How do you want to feel? What do you dream about doing, being, having?

Make sure to specifically answer these questions:

- Where are you working?

- How do you work with your clients, customers or patients?

- Do you work: online, offline, or a mix of both?

- How much are you interacting with clients, customers or patients? 1:1? In groups? Not at all?

- Do you have a team, colleagues, coworkers?

- What other work activities do you do? Writing books? Speaking? Retreats? Workshops? Online Courses? A Podcast? TV appearances? What would make up your ultimate work life?

Don't let yourself get stuck here. You don't need to figure out *exactly* what your business and life are going to look like (after all, that's pretty much impossible). What you want is to identify how you want to feel, and the values that will influence your life and business. There are no right or wrong answers, and you can change and evolve this vision over time. Just be as specific as possible about what you want right now, and know it's going to evolve.

Now that you have the rough outline of your ideal life and business, the next step is to make a visual representation of where you're going.

These are often called vision boards, but you don't need to be "woo-woo" or believe in manifestation to use them. Creating a vision board for your life and business is useful because looking at it helps you instantly refocus on your goals and what's important to you.

Rather than writing about your ideal life, a vision board lets you reconnect with your vision at a glance, so you can get re-aligned and back on the right path when you're overwhelmed or distracted. You can add words to your vision board too if it helps — it can be in whatever format feels good for you. Keep it in a prominent location (in your office or even as your computer desktop background) so you see it regularly.

Exercise: Create Your Vision Board

The traditional way to make a vision board is very low tech: with a big stack of magazines, scissors and glue. But if you're more digitally inclined, you can create a digital collage and set it as your computer desktop background image.

The key with a vision board is keeping it somewhere you can see everyday (ideally, multiple times per day). I love having my board as my laptop desktop background — I'm on my computer so much it's easy to get re-centered at any time!

Here's the process that I use to make my vision board. (I do this about three times per year, or whenever I feel like my vision has grown and I'm ready for something bigger.)

Start with the visualizing and free-writing exercises above to identify the key words and concepts that you want to create in your life and business.

Then you'll either create a physical (paper) or digital vision board.

For the physical version, get a thick sheet of paper that will work as your board (or you could just get a bulletin or cork board and pin the pictures to it). Get a stack of magazines and flip through them, cutting out words and pictures that attract you.

Don't think too hard — just go for what attracts you, and represents what you want to create in your life and business. Glue them onto the paper in any way that feels good. Personally, I start with photos, and tend to rip the edges (rather than cutting them) to make them look more natural, overlapping images and letting them hang off the edge of the paper (you can always trim it later if you want).

I finish with the words, and put the words over and around the images. You can cut out the words, or simply write them with markers and paint. It's a creative process and it's your vision board — you can do it however you like!

If you want a digital version, you can collect pictures from around the internet and use a photo editing tool to make a collage (see the Book Bonuses for my current recommendation). I recommend saving it as a JPEG and then setting it as your desktop background or printing it out.

(Note: Only use images from the internet if you plan to keep your vision board private, for personal use only. It is NOT OK to use images from the internet on your website or even social media that don't belong to you — buy Royalty Free images, or take your own pictures!)

Now the magic step — hang it where you can see it easily. If this technique is going to work for you — make it EASY. Where can you put your vision board so that you see it several times per day? In your office? Or what about in your kitchen, or beside your bed so you see it first thing when you wake up and before you go to sleep? When I lived in London, I hung my vision board on the bulletin board beside my desk. Currently it's my laptop desktop background image. Anytime you feel overwhelmed or lost or caught up in the details of running your business, just take a deep breath and look at your vision board for a few seconds to reconnect with where you're going.

If you'd like more help with creating a vision for your business and life, I've recommended some additional resources in the Book Bonuses (WellpreneurBook.com/bonus).

ACTION STEPS:

- Do the visualization and free-writing exercises to clarify what you'd like to create in your life and business.

- Create your vision board, and hang it where you can see it daily.

- Share a picture of your vision board with the hashtag #wellpreneurbook.

Amanda Cook

Wellpreneur Interview: Kimberly Wilson

Kimberly Wilson is a writer, therapist, yogi and creative entrepreneur who founded Tranquil Space in Washington, DC, named among the top 25 yoga studios in the world by Travel + Leisure. In this interview, she shares how she expanded her business vision from a single yoga studio to a brand that encompasses books, online courses, retreats, clothing and a non-profit. Learn more about Kimberly at KimberlyWilson.com.

I was working as a trademark paralegal in my mid-20s and had become a bit disenchanted with the idea of the American dream. I enjoyed my work, but I didn't feel fulfilled. I didn't like the idea that I had to do this for 40 more years until I could travel and have fun in retirement! There had to be a better way.

Soon after that, I started a yoga studio in my living room. This was back in 1999 before yoga was popular in Washington DC. I didn't know much about business — I was interested in creating community, a place in a big city where people would feel a part of something bigger. That was the beginning of Tranquil Space.

I think the key to success is to know your core focus. For me, it started as yoga, and now is the brand Tranquility. Everything I do relates to that. Now we have two physical locations and serve about 1,500 yogis per week with a team of over 100 teachers. In 2002, I launched the clothing line Tranquility. I created the clothing line to solve a problem I had in my life. I wanted something I could wear to teach yoga and then go out on a date, but still look put together. Since then, I've also written several books, launched our non-profit, the Tranquil Space Foundation, and I also run a podcast, a blog, and online courses.

I think it's really important to be able to take little trajectories to follow your interests. Not going down rabbit holes, but just expanding and exploring based on your interests. As long as it comes back to a core focus, it will all make sense. I didn't originally plan to create all of these parts of Tranquility. They evolved over time from my interests — like being in love with Paris, or wanting a clothing line that didn't exist.

I really encourage new entrepreneurs to think about how to expand beyond the four walls of your business. I started with a physical yoga studio, but was able to expand through the blog, podcast, online courses and even retreats in Paris and Provence. And that's been great because the majority of people who take those online programs are not local to us in DC. I think that is really amazing. Online can have such a huge reach. It is a wonderful way to deepen your work, and impact people around the world!

Listen to the complete interview in the Book Bonuses:
WellpreneurBook.com/bonus

Chapter 2

Nail Your Niche

"Don't ask what the world needs. Ask what makes you come alive, and go do it. Because what the world needs is people who have come alive."

— Howard Thurman

Oh, the infamous "target market". I'm guessing you've been told (probably more than once!) that you must choose a target market before you start marketing.

It's one of the first instructions from the mouths of marketers because it's true: if you try to market to everyone, you market to no one.

But it's not just new business owners who struggle to define their target market (also called a *niche*.) Even when I work with established wellness businesses or corporate clients, we still revisit and refine their target market again and again. We do it for each campaign, each product, each email broadcast. So don't rush through this section, even if you feel like you know your ideal customer already. You can always gain a deeper level of understanding, to improve your marketing, products and client relationships.

Many wellpreneurs are resistant to choosing a target market. But I can tell you from experience that it is crucial that you identify a target market before you start marketing your business online. Sure, you can start building a following randomly based upon who likes your most recent blog posts. But if you're *ultimately trying to sell things to your audience* then you'll reach your goal much faster if you choose a specific target market up front.

 This chapter is a sticking point for many wellpreneurs. You may think you're not ready to pick a target market, or that you don't want to cut off your options, or that it doesn't apply to your kind of business. I disagree. If you want the rest of your marketing to be effective, it's essential to do this step. Don't skip it.

Target Market Myths

When I ask new wellpreneurs to choose a target market, I hear two objections repeatedly.

1) "My product or service can help everyone! Picking a target market would eliminate 95% of my potential customers."

2) "Choosing a target market feels so permanent. I don't want to be stuck in this little box forever!"

Let's debunk these myths, and then I'll share my new approach to a target market that feels freeing and helps you move forward quickly.

1) "My product or service can help everyone! Picking a target market will eliminate 95% of my potential customers."

First, let's get clear about the purpose of a target market.

A target market defines *who you market to*. It's not a limit on who you work with.

If you meet a potential customer who is outside your target market, but you want to work with her — go right ahead! The role of marketing is not to limit who can buy your products and services, but to attract ideal new customers to your business.

Think back to the last time you had a problem with your health or wellbeing when you actively searched for a solution. Did you want a one-size-fits-all solution that could work for you, your spouse, a toddler, your great uncle Harry, and the elderly woman who lives across town? Or did you want a specific solution that fixed your problem, *for people like you*, with success stories *from people like you*, and with tips, advice and strategies *specifically for your situation.*

You wanted the specific solution, right? Without knowing anything more about the programs, it feels so much more credible. It feels like a safer bet. The specific solution implies that the company knows people like you, and has helped people like you before, so you feel confident it will probably work for you too. Whereas the generic product — who knows? Did the people it worked for also have full-time jobs and families? Were they also gluten-intolerant? Were they also paleo or vegan? Who knows! It's generic, so it seems less credible.

Amanda Cook

Generic offerings raise too many questions in your customer's mind, and create doubt about whether your solution will work *in her specific situation*.

Let's look at another example:

Imagine you're a holistic health coach who helps people transition to a whole foods diet. You know your clients will experience improvements in their skin, look younger, boost their energy, lose weight, stabilize their blood sugar levels, get stronger hair and nails, and fewer food cravings, just to mention a few possible outcomes. And who would like those outcomes? Almost everyone eating a typical western diet!

But imagine if that was your marketing: "Hire me as your health coach and you'll lose weight, have more energy, have better skin, hair and nails, look younger and stabilize your blood sugar! My solution works for everyone — teenagers, men, new moms, menopausal women, diabetics, vegans, broke college students, jet-setting playboys and busy professionals!"

Would you buy a product like that? I wouldn't. It sounds like a miracle pill or snake oil!

When you encounter marketing like that, your BS detector immediately activates and you think: *"Can it really do all those things? How can it work for everyone? It sounds too good to be true."*

Even if you overcome those initial objections, then this type of marketing raises new questions:

"But can it help me? After all, I'm busy/broke/gluten-free/vegan/hate vegetables/won't exercise/ live in Antarctica/can't cook — will it work for people like me?"

At this rate, you will spend all day answering the questions that your marketing has raised and never making it to a sale.

Or more likely, you'll just hear crickets from your marketing. Total radio silence. No inquiries, no enthusiastic sharing of your products and services, and no clients.

When you have a very specific offering, your target customer instantly connects with you and wants to hear what you have to say:

- "I'm a health coach who works with new moms to get their pre-baby figures back in six months."

- "I help athletes maintain lean muscle mass and performance on a vegan diet."

- "I help busy executives to reduce their stress levels and increase productivity."

So — don't worry at all about limiting yourself by choosing a target market. With online marketing, you'll see faster results by being super specific about who you work with.

Amanda Cook

2) "Choosing a target market feels so permanent. I don't want to be stuck in this little box forever!"

If you choose new moms as your target market, are you destined to work with them forever? What about your equally fervent passion for supporting endurance athletes and 20-something newlyweds?

If you become known as the 'detox' girl, what happens to your skills in personal training or meditation?

Getting stuck in a target market is a really common concern, and I will just tell you right now — don't worry about it. Pick a target market and move forward.

Here's why: there is no way you can predict what direction your business is going to take as it grows. Your clients will change, you will change, and the products and services you offer will change.

The point of choosing a target market is to get traction in a single market. By focusing all of your marketing efforts into one target market, you'll see results a lot more quickly than spreading yourself across five potential markets. And once you have clients (and revenue!) coming in through this one market, you have a choice. You can choose to stick with your one focused target market and continue to grow your revenue, or you could choose to expand into a second target market, because now you have money and time to invest in it. But if you try to be everything to everyone from the beginning, you won't have the clients or revenue to grow in *any* of the markets.

So choose one target market and move forward.

To make it easy, I've got a simple method for choosing a target market for your business, and it's different than anything you've done before…

Introducing: The Six-Month Target Market

I started using The Six-Month Target Market approach with my clients because I saw too many of them getting stuck and stressed about choosing a target market.

Rather than putting intense pressure on yourself to find the 'perfect' target market for your business to serve forever (which is an impossible task, if I've ever heard one), let's shift our thinking.

With the Six-Month Target Market, you're committing to pursue this specific target market completely and with 100% focus for the next six months.

If the market is going to respond to your offer, you'll start to see traction within the first six months — if you focus on it consistently. This traction shows up as a growing email list, increased web traffic, social media likes and shares, engagement with your audience and of course, clients and revenue.

At the end of the six months, you'll have three options:

1. **Grow:** You're enthusiastic about your market and it's getting results, so you put more resources into it to go bigger and generate more revenue with what you're already doing.

2. **Expand:** You still like the market and it's getting results, but you see an opportunity in a related space, so you add a second target market to grow in the next six months.

3. **Change:** You decide you don't like this market, or that it's not working for you, and you change to something else.

Although six months may feel like a long time to stick with one thing — in the big picture of your business and life, it goes by in a flash. I often see wellpreneurs making the critical mistake of not giving an online marketing tactic enough time to get any traction, before dropping it and moving onto something else. Give it time to see what's going to work for your business.

When you switch between target markets, you lose **the follow-through, focus and commitment to really get to know your ideal customers and serve their needs.**

So, choosing a Six-Month Target Market can be fun and easy. It's not forever. And it's NOT your entire business! In fact, it's just the first path to turn website visitors into paying clients that you'll create in your growing business.

Let's look at an example of the Six-Month Target Market in action:

Say you help new moms to get more and better sleep. You launch a program or service to help them sleep, you build a community of new moms, and you start to see some sales of your program. After six months of total focus on the new mom market, you have a choice. Maybe you're really loving this market and see lots of potential, so you double down on growing your business there. Or you might decide that the new mom market is ticking along nicely, and you want to add a new market of college students who also aren't sleeping well. The key takeaway is that you can't start both of these things at once. **You must choose ONE first, and build it out for at least six months to see results — before deciding if you want to open an additional market. Otherwise, you're on the fast-track to online business burnout.**

Exercise: Choose Your Six-Month Target Market

Get something to write with, and let yourself free-write a long list of potential target markets as you ask yourself these questions:

- Who do you feel drawn to help?

- What type of people do you love to work with?

- What health or wellness challenges have you overcome yourself?

- What types of clients (or people) are already in your life?

- What groups of people are you a part of?

Now take a break for at least 15 minutes (I suggest getting some fresh air or exercise to clear your head).

Then review each of the groups on your paper, and eliminate any which don't meet the following criteria:

- I'm excited about working with people in this group. *(If you get any sense of 'ugh' or a sinking feeling — cross them off the list! If you're indifferent, or feel like you should work with them just because you know about their problems, remove them from the list too!)*

- My products or services can help people in this group.

- People in this group have money to spend on my products or services (you can help people with very tight budgets, but I don't recommend very budget-conscious groups for your first target market).

- I have access to some people in this group, or I know where I can find them.

By now you probably have a few groups left on your paper. If all of the groups meet the four criteria above, then just go with the one you're most excited about at this point in your business. What's your gut feeling on this? Which of those groups feels the easiest and most fun? Remember, it's just for six months, and then you can adjust. Choose your Six-Month Target Market now.

Examples of good and bad target markets:

Bad target markets (because they're too vague):
everyone, women, men, retirees, athletes, stressed out people, people concerned about their health, people who want to lose weight, women 20-50.

Good target markets (because they're clear and specific):
moms of teenagers, professional women who don't sleep well, new moms who want their figure back, empty-nesters who are re-establishing their relationship, singles over 40 who want to get married, 30-something women with IBS, men with eczema, overweight 20-somethings in Boston, gluten-free couples without children, vegan weightlifters, first-time triathletes, etc.

Again, let's remember: this is not your entire business — this is just your first path towards converting website visitors into paying clients! You can and will evolve your business and this market over time, so be as specific as possible now.

The final step is to commit to this target market for six months.

Take your calendar, and flip to the date six months from today. Put an entry for "Six-Month Target Market Complete — Review + Celebrate!"

ACTION STEPS:

- Use the exercise in this chapter to pick your Six-Month Target Market. Commit for six months. Write it down!

- Set a date on your calendar to reevaluate your Six-Month Target Market.

Amanda Cook

Wellpreneur Interview: Lacey Baier

Lacey Baier is the founder of A Sweet Pea Chef, and teaches healthy, easy, and family-friendly home cooking. In this interview, she shares why trying to sell her products before getting to know her customers was a mistake. Learn more at ASweetPeaChef.com.

I started the blog around the in-person personal chef business I was running. But then we moved out of state, and I was going to have to start over finding in-person personal chef clients, so I decided to focus on the blog instead.

Suddenly there was all this pressure to make money from my blog. I was working on it with my husband — I'd do the writing and photography and he'd handle the tech side. We decided to create a free downloadable cookbook. At that time, five years ago, not many food blogs had done that, so we gained a lot of subscribers. Then we decided to create an eBook for sale. I really thought that would be it! That one eBook was going to be a sustainable business so the blog could be my full-time job... I think we only sold $300 worth of the eBook.

Looking back on it, I should've been so stoked that I'd turned nothing into something of value. But at the time I felt so deflated because we'd spent so much time on it — it had taken months to create! It was scary that we would spend so much time on something and have it flop.

But we kept going and trying new things. I was home working on the blog while my husband had a full-time job. At night he would help me with everything. We felt like we were pulling our hair out, trying everything possible to make money. At one point it just became too much. I wanted to just archive it and go back to work. But looking back, we were trying to put the carriage before the horse, trying to make money before actually solving anyone's problems!

The turning point came through in our personal life. We started eating a clean, whole foods diet and exercising more. Soon the blog felt out of alignment, because we were sharing recipes for cinnamon rolls, but in our personal lives we didn't eat that anymore!

It caused a lot of soul-searching at that time. Ultimately we had to pivot our brand into something we were passionate about that we felt we could do for the long haul. That's what really started us growing. We built an audience around healthy eating and healthy living, and then we started solving their problems. When you can find something that solves that problem for the audience, the money-making part is going to be a lot easier.

What I love about working for myself online is that you're constantly able to find new ways to reach people, help people and keep growing and improving.

Listen to the complete interview in the Book Bonuses:
WellpreneurBook.com/bonus

Chapter 3

Finding the Problem to Solve

"You can have everything you want in life if you just help enough people get what they want in life."

– Zig Ziglar

Now that you know your target market, what results are you going to help them achieve?

The most effective online marketing helps a specific person achieve a specific result.

Unfortunately, it gets a little complicated in the wellness industry, because there are so many paths and modalities to wellbeing! And the vast majority of people have no idea what any of it means.

Most people don't know the difference between a holistic health coach, EFT practitioner, or Bowen therapist, and they definitely don't know what problems these wellpreneurs could help them solve.

Similarly, people don't know the details of being vegan, paleo, whole foods, or plant-based, or whether they should do food combining, the Blood Type diet or avoid wheat. *"What do these labels even mean... and more importantly, can they even solve my problem?"*

Wellpreneurs, on the other hand, become extremely passionate about THEIR path to wellness, and forget that most people have absolutely no clue what they're talking about.

That's why relying on your official job title or profession, saying that you're an "iridologist who works with busy women" doesn't give much clarity about how you actually help your clients. Don't make the mistake of assuming that if you state your title, people will know what you do.

(There are some exceptions for wellness modalities that have gone mainstream, such as chiropractic or yoga, but you still want to use the strategies in this chapter to differentiate yourself from your competition and attract YOUR ideal clients to your business.)

Since you're not going to use your job title to attract the right clients to your business, here's where you need to get super specific (again!) about HOW you can help your Six-Month Target Market.

Not only will this make your marketing language more clear, but it also makes it much more effective, because your target market will *feel like you're speaking specifically to them*, addressing *their* problems and *their* dreams.

When you can identify a few specific problems that you solve for your specific target market, you'll find it so much easier to get clients because people understand exactly how you can help them.

This raises another common objection: "I help my clients with lots of areas of their life — not just one problem!" You're right. This one specific problem you're choosing to solve isn't your entire business. It doesn't encompass all of your capabilities as a wellpreneur. And it's certainly not the only area where your clients will experience results. But your marketing needs to be clear, focused and easy to understand in just a few seconds. So we're going to choose one major problem to focus on marketing for (you guessed it!) the next six months.

Let's return to the previous example of the wellpreneur who helps new moms to get more and better sleep.

After six months, you have an established community of moms and success stories from your program. Now you're ready to grow into something new. But instead of choosing an additional target market, you speak with your community and uncover more of their needs. Your community members tell you that they're also struggling with putting healthy meals on the table while trying to care for the baby. That's an area you know you can help with, so you create a new program or service to help new moms prepare quick and healthy meals. It's a natural extension of your brand because you're serving the same market — and as a bonus — you've already got a list and an engaged community, so it's easy to test out new product offerings.

Your task in this chapter is to choose one specific problem that you can solve for your one specific target market.

As you know, because of the integrated nature of holistic health, everything is connected. That means that if you make a change or improvement in one area, you'll likely see results in multiple areas. This is fantastic from a health and lifestyle perspective, but not so good from a marketing perspective. So what do you talk about in your marketing? Which problems do you try to solve, when in reality, every area of their life might change after working with you?

You'll find the best problems to solve by coming at it from two directions: Your perspective and their perspective.

First let's tackle the easy one, your perspective. Just make a big list of all the problems you know you can help your Six-Month Target Market with. It'll probably be a big list.

Second, let's dig into THEIR perspective of their problems. This is where the solid gold lies in your marketing.

At first you'll *assume* that you know their problems. (Who among us doesn't hear someone complaining about their health and think, "Well if they'd just _____, it'd be fixed!"?) And you *might* know some of their problems, but I can almost guarantee you that you do not know their specific problems *in their specific words*.

Why?

Because as experts, we are NOT part of our target market.

Even if you are part of the same demographic, you're not part of that target market anymore, because you have expertise in the area where they're struggling.

That means you think differently from them about this issue. Your understanding of the problem, your identification of the cause, the solutions and possibilities you see, the words you use to describe the problem...They're all different from your ideal customer.

And if you don't use HER own words (the words of your ideal customer), then you'll never convince her to buy from you, because she won't understand what you're offering, or won't think she has a need.

Let's take a simplistic example. Imagine you have a client who is always hungry and snacks throughout the day.

You, as the wellness expert, immediately realize that she could have a problem with inconsistent blood sugar, and needs to eat more protein and fat, and dramatically reduce sugar in her diet. But if you sell a program or service to talk about stabilizing blood sugar or going 'sugar-free', she won't buy it.

Why not?

Because she doesn't know that's her problem!

Your ideal client is actually on Google searching for 'healthy snacks to stay full between meals' or 'low calorie healthy snacks' so she can keep eating all day without gaining weight. You're speaking a different language!

This is one of the major reasons wellness practitioners struggle to get clients — because they're speaking a different language from their clients.

It may not be as extreme as doctors using medical jargon, but in the wellness world, we have our own jargon and make assumptions about how much people already know. Here are some things to keep in mind:

- Most people are beginners.

- Most people get their health and wellness information from TV shows or random social media posts.

- Most people have no idea what you do, or the root cause of their problem — they've got a symptom, it's causing them pain, and they want to fix it!

So it's up to you, Wellpreneur, to uncover what your client thinks her problems are, What does SHE think is keeping her stuck from reaching her ideal health? What is she frustrated about with her health, wellness or life? What is she actually Googling to try to fix her problem?

You're looking for the overlap between the problems you can solve, and the problems she thinks she has.

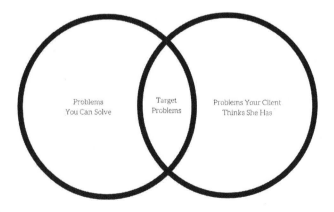

It's time to become a marketing detective.

So how do you find out what problems your ideal client thinks she has?

There's one effective way to do this, and a bunch of ineffective ways.

The quickest and most effective way is just to ask her. To get a real potential customer on the phone, and ask her questions about her frustrations, her dreams, what she's tried before and what's worked (or not).

This can feel scary, because you can't hide behind your computer (which is so easy to do with an online business) and you actually have to find some potential customers and get them on the phone. But this is the fastest way to identify with your ideal customer and figure out what key problems you can solve for her, and to hear her talk about her problems in her own language.

You are going to want to skip this part. I know, because everyone wants to skip this part. I want to skip this part every time I do it! You'll think you know enough about what your market needs and you'll just want to pick a problem and move on. But do so at your own risk. Nothing bad will happen, but nothing good will happen either. You'll waste a lot of time creating emails and blogs and products and services and sales pages without many sales... and eventually you'll come around to doing these market research phone calls anyway because they're the fastest way to identify the right problem and get clear, effective marketing language. So just try a few calls, and save yourself the time and frustration. You might be surprised at what you learn!

The goal of this exercise is to understand *what the customer thinks her problems are*. We also want to understand her frustrations in this area of her life, how these problems impact other areas of her life (like her relationships, her job, her health etc.) and what would change if the problem was resolved. We'd also like to know what she's tried before, and other experts she looks to for information on this topic.

At this point, many wellpreneurs try to avoid doing market research calls by simply running a survey. These can work and I've done them myself, but they're still less effective than getting on the phone. Here's why:

1) A survey is most effective when you have a bigger audience (at least 500 subscribers — or you just won't get enough replies for it to be useful).

2) People write differently than they speak. Since part of the goal of this research is to capture the exact words that your ideal clients use, you want to hear them talk about their problems. People write differently — either they write more "academically," or they write in short abbreviated sentences, or they only write the bare minimum because it was a required survey question.

3) There's a huge risk of getting stuck at the analysis phase. If you did get 100 survey responses back, what would you do with that data? Analyzing bulk data like this can send a lot of wellpreneurs into math-class anxiety or deep boredom, so they don't do it at all!

Another approach to figure out your target market's problems is by doing a ton of research. You could look at magazines and blogs targeting that same audience and see what they're writing about. What are people asking in the comments? You could go into online forums to see what people are asking or answering. You could ask lots of questions in social media groups and collate your answers. But again, this is a lot of effort, and you're still left with lots of data that you need to analyze. Not fun.

So we're back to the market research phone calls. These are quick and easy (15-20 minutes per person), and have the added bonus of building a real connection and relationship with a potential customer — which can only help you in the future!

Exercise: Market Research Calls

Challenge yourself to do at least 10 research calls with members of your target market.

You can invite people you know personally, current or former clients, friends-of-friends, social media contacts, any existing email subscribers you have — anyone, as long as they fit into your target market.

You want to be really clear that this is a market research interview, not a sales call!

One summer I did 40 of these calls. I emailed my list to share that I was creating a new program, and wanted to tailor it exactly for their problems and challenges. Then I asked for volunteers to do a short 15 minute phone interview with me so I could understand their frustrations and tailor the program to them. The response was fantastic. I had over 50 people agree to be interviewed, and managed to actually speak with 40 of them. People love to help, and also love to be a part of something new. Plus, if an expert were going to create a product or service *exactly to meet your needs*, wouldn't you want to help them get it right?

And, as an unexpected benefit, most interviewees reported that the call was helpful for them as well! Simply having an expert listen attentively as they explained their problem and how it was impacting their life helped them to work through the issue themselves. So it was a win-win 15 minutes for everyone.

Here's my simple formula for effective market research calls:

1. Be the leader.

Greet the interviewee and thank them for doing the call with you. Then set the ground rules: it's a 15-minute call, and the purpose is to interview them about their problems and frustrations around their _____ (health, weight, strength training, skin, sleep — whatever your list of potential problems to solve might be), so you can tailor your upcoming program to their needs. Say that you'll ask them a specific series of questions, and because you have limited time, if you get off-track, you'll gently bring the conversation back to the questions. Is that OK with them? Yes? Great!

2. Write down key words and phrases the client says during the call.

As the client is speaking, write down the *exact words and phrases* she uses to talk about her problem. Don't transcribe the whole conversation — just write down the key words and phrases about the problem and its impact on her life.

3. FIRST QUESTION: What are your three biggest frustrations with _____ ?

Depending on how much your interviewee talks, this might take one minute or could take the entire call! If they only briefly state their three frustrations, or if you want more detail and descriptive language, draw them out by saying "You mentioned that _____ was a frustration, can you tell me more about that?" Do NOT say something like "Oh, you mentioned that cravings are a frustration, are you eating a lot of sugar?" That is a leading question and you're putting words in their mouth. Remember, we are here to capture *their* words. You want to ask open-ended, general questions, and get them talking. Plus, this is NOT a coaching call, you're not here to fix anything — this is a market research interview!

4. SECOND QUESTION: If I could wave a magic wand and fix (the three frustrations they mentioned above), what would change in your life?

The goal of this question is to get at the EMOTION behind the problem. How is their life being impacted by this problem? It's often far beyond a simple health concern, and often extends into their relationships, work and self-worth.

5. THIRD QUESTION (if you have time): What have you tried so far to fix the problem? What experts or websites do you visit to learn about the problem?

These questions can tell you what types of solutions people are searching for, and which experts, websites or blogs could be a good source of potential clients.

6. Wrap up.

Thank them for their time and ask if it's OK if you get back in touch with them when your new product/program/service launches. (They'll say yes, and then you have an excuse to follow up with them and offer them your new product!)

As tempting as it might be — *talk as little as possible on these calls*, and definitely do not start coaching the client or trying to solve their problem. You've been upfront that this is a market research interview, and you will benefit much more from listening to the client with an open mind, rather than trying to think of solutions for them or trying to sell them your services! If they want your help, they can hire you.

After you've done at least five calls, you'll start to see patterns and words that appear again and again.

You don't need to do any major analysis, as you'll have a good gut feeling at this point about what the major problems are for your market.

So which of those problems can you either solve, or help them along to the next step on their journey?

Write out each of the problems that you can help with, along with *the exact words and phrases* your potential clients used. You'll want to save these notes, as you'll come back to them over and over again as you're building out your marketing.

Now it's time to choose your focus problem. You might have a gut feeling at this point about which problem you want to solve. Pick the biggest, most frustrating problem for your target market — what is keeping them up at night? What's so painful that they'll pay for a solution for it?

It should be a problem that re-appeared across multiple potential clients, and should be a problem you know you can solve.

Remember: this is just the one problem that you are solving for this specific market for the next six months.

Let's wrap up this step by writing out a statement of your Six-Month Target Market and the problem you solve.

Write this sentence for your own target market and the main problem you solve:

"I help <target market> to fix <main problem> so that they can <result>."

You might say...

- I help new moms sleep better so that they can care for their families and themselves.

- I help women transition through menopause, so that they feel sexy, strong, and centered.

- I help corporate executives to fuel their bodies so that they perform at peak everyday.

- I help marathon runners transition to a vegan diet without sacrificing performance or the planet.

- I prepare healthy meals for busy families, so their fridge is always stocked with nourishing tasty food without having to go to the grocery store!

Feel free to adjust the sentence to fit your business. The idea is to have a single, clear statement that says who you help, the problem you solve and the benefit the client gets out of it. Write it out your Six-Month Target Market statement now. (You might consider adding this statement to your vision board too.)

ACTION STEPS:

- Challenge yourself to conduct at least 10 market research interviews with people in your target market in the next two weeks!

- Review your notes from these calls, and identify the one problem you are going to focus on solving in the next six months.

- Write down your commitment: Until (date six months from now) I commit to helping (target audience) solve (the problem).

Wellpreneur Interview: Darya Rose, PhD

Darya Rose is a neuroscience PhD, author, former dieter, proud foodist and founder of Summer Tomato. In this interview, she shares how she engages with her audience to discover what products and programs to create. Learn more about Darya at SummerTomato.com.

I thought I was going to be a research scientist in neuroscience. I was a couple years into my PhD program, and I was starting to get really disillusioned with the whole academic world.

I was always into fitness and health and specifically dieting. I grew up in Southern California during the Baywatch era, and I was always struggling to be thinner. At some point, I realized that I had enough training in science that I could figure it out on my own, because everything I'd tried over the last 15 years was a short-term fix that made me miserable.

So I decided to try a weird plan I created based on the data — it sounded so non-scientific, but it was what the data was telling me, and it was a complete life transformation for me. I was eating real food with flavor for the first time of my life. I discovered the farmer's market and I started to cook. I realized the diet industry was trying to sell us crappy products and we should be shopping at the farmer's market.

So I started exploring food writing and journalism, and then ultimately found blogging. I put myself on a very rigorous blogging schedule. I was blogging Monday, Wednesday, and Friday. By the time my thesis was done and I graduated, I had this whole other career.

Amanda Cook

The first thing I did to make money through my blog was put ads on it. And I made about 10 cents a day! That really didn't work. A lot of bloggers do sponsorships, but that never felt right to me. I wanted to be able to write whatever I wanted, without having to show certain products in a good light. Then I tried a paid newsletter for $3.99 per month. People signed up to that, but it wasn't enough to pay the bills. Ultimately, I decided to create my own programs, and that was the turning point for me.

One problem I see on newer blogs is that the author acts like a know-it-all, as if they have all of the answers. Honestly, you don't have all of the answers. You have ideas, theories and stories, but you need to be super honest with your audience about what works and what doesn't work. And more importantly, you have to listen to them when they say it doesn't work for them. Don't tell them why they're wrong. Listen and really get to the bottom of it. It's not going to be a simple answer. It's easy to have a reflex to just tell people what to do. But if you really listen, and your audience knows you listen, and you reflect it back to them, are compassionate with them and give them real talk and real answers, they will respect you and they will go to the ends of the earth to help you.

If you listen enough, you start to hear patterns. That's why I started a cooking program. Honestly, it was never my goal in life to teach people how to make stir-fried cauliflower. But my goal in life is to get people healthy, and I heard over and over again that the people who were struggling weren't cooking. And then I listened even more and learned that the recipe was the bottleneck.

So then I got on the phone with people from my audience and asked them all about it. All different types of people from my audience, to really try to understand their challenges and their perspective. And *then* I created a program. That's why my programs work, because I'm clear on how it can help them!

Listen to the complete interview in the Book Bonuses: WellpreneurBook.com/bonus

Chapter 4

Digital Products and Services

"I have learned never to ask whether you can do something. Say, instead, that you are doing it. Then fasten your seat belt. The most remarkable things follow."

— Julia Cameron

At this point, you've got a clear idea of who your ideal customer is and what problems you can solve for them. But what, exactly, are you going to sell them?

You can use the marketing system I teach in this book to sell anything: in-person services, physical products, online coaching, downloadable eBooks or complete video courses, to name a few options. But in this chapter, I want to encourage you to include one or more digital products in your business.

A digital product is a product that's completely delivered online, such as an eBook, video course or online group coaching program. Every wellpreneur can add digital products to their business, even if you provide an in-person therapy like massage, acupuncture or yoga. Digital products can be your entire business, or simply provide an additional income stream. They're flexible, relatively quick and low-cost to create, and can be used in multiple ways in your business. For example, you could use digital products as:

- A free promotional tool to let potential customers experience your work.

- A bonus gift when purchasing another product or service.

- A supplement to your existing products and services. For example, a nutrition coach could offer a digital recipe book. A yoga studio could offer online video classes for students to use while they're travelling.

- Your primary business, selling digital products alone or in bundles.

And digital products are easier to create than you might think. Once you understand the basic types of digital products, you can let your creativity flow to figure out the right combination and branding to fit your business.

The key to success with digital products is to start small, get feedback, and iterate.

I learned this lesson the hard way.

My first digital product was a course teaching wellpreneurs how to build WordPress websites. I was getting lots of requests to create websites, and since I didn't want to start a web development business, I decided to create a course to teach people how to build a website themselves, and spent three months creating it. I filmed videos and step-by-step screenshare walkthroughs. I made handouts and worksheets. I gave and gave and gave valuable information inside the course... And then I tried to sell it.

The results were underwhelming at best. Before spending so long creating the course, I had skipped the step of validating *if my people actually wanted to buy a course like this*. And it turned out that most of them didn't. A handful of courses sold, but it didn't compensate me for the huge amount of time and effort I had spent creating the course! In retrospect, the majority of serious wellpreneurs will pay to have a professional create their website. And the wellpreneurs who didn't want to pay for web development also didn't want to pay for a WordPress course! Although I got great feedback from my few customers, this experience really knocked me around. I'd spent so much time, effort and a bit of money getting the course ready, and it really wasn't right for my market.

You now know that what I should have done *before* creating my program was a series of market research calls with potential customers, like we discussed in the previous chapter. Then I could have created a quick and simple beta version of the course and run a live version to get feedback and testimonials while I was building it. THEN after I had success stories and lots of feedback, I could decide if I wanted to turn it into a nicely packaged online course.

Looking back, it seems so obvious. But at the time, I was just eager to create something and launch it to the world! So as you're thinking about which digital products you want to create, I urge you: start simply, get feedback and iterate.

Five Digital Products for Wellness Businesses

The basic components of a digital product are text, audio and video. You can include one or more of these, it's up to you.

Here are some examples of what you could include in a digital product:

- **Text:** eBook or guide, worksheets, PDFs, templates, checklists, shopping lists.

- **Audio:** Interviews, lectures, meditations, podcasts etc.

- **Video:** how-to videos (exercise, cooking etc), video lectures or lessons, video interviews, tours etc.

Sometimes digital products also include interactive elements such as:

- **Group or Forum:** this is often a Facebook group or private forum for people who have purchased the program to connect with each other and ask questions.

- **Live group or 1:1 calls:** often conducted through a video conferencing service like Skype or Zoom.

You can combine these elements in numerous ways to create a digital product that fits your business. The details of how to create each type of digital product are beyond the scope of this book. Instead, I want to give you an idea of the types of digital products you could create to get your creativity flowing for how to use these products in your business. Let's keep it simple, and look at the five most common types of digital products for your wellness business:

1. eBook

When I say "eBook" you might think about the hugely complicated effort to *write a book* and get it published. Not so! Many eBooks are simply downloadable PDFs, and often much shorter than a full book. You could create an eBook of recipes, a step-by-step plan, or a short guide on a specific subject. There's no reason to wait until you can write an entire book to have an eBook on your website!

eBooks are brilliant as a first digital product because they're inexpensive, quick to produce, easy to download and people know what they are. They also provide a low-cost entry point for customers to start to work with you.

The drawback of eBooks is that your ideal customer might forget she downloaded it and never read your great advice and tips. (You might have done this yourself with other people's eBooks!) We'll talk more about how to ensure your potential customer reads your eBook in the Nurture + Convert chapter.

2. Toolkit

A Toolkit goes beyond an eBook and provides actionable items like worksheets, checklists, templates and possibly how-to videos to help your client achieve a goal.

A health coach, nutritionist or healthy chef could easily put together a healthy shopping toolkit including a recipe guide, shopping list, resource guide of your favorite places to buy healthy foods, and a few videos demonstrating your favorite recipes or cooking techniques.

A personal trainer might create a toolkit including workout videos, resource lists for where to buy gear or supplements, fitness tracking worksheets etc.

Depending on what you include, a toolkit can have a much higher perceived value than an eBook because it is more actionable.

3. Simple Email Course

This is my favorite kind of digital product for new wellpreneurs because it's so easy to create.

A Simple Email Course is delivered completely through email. You'll often see this type of course positioned as a week-long, 10-day or 30-day program, sometimes called a "challenge."

The basic format is that your client signs up for the course (which can be free or paid), and they're added to a special email distribution list for that course. Then they're sent the course materials in installments (maybe daily or weekly) by email. You might write the course material directly in the email, or more typically include it as a PDF download or a video.

I love the Simple Email Course for two reasons:

1) It breaks your content down into bite-sized pieces that are easy for the customer to consume. You can provide the same content you would in an eBook, but in a more actionable format, delivered over several days or weeks.

2) Because you're regularly delivering valuable content to your customers, it builds your relationship with them, and provides multiple points for engagement and interaction.

You can run a Simple Email Course as a paid program, or as a free promotional tool to build your email list. You'll often see wellpreneurs running this type of program as a "Free Challenge" over a week or 10 days. We'll talk about this more in Chapter 7 about your email opt-in gift.

4. Online Course

You're probably familiar with Online Courses — maybe you've taken one yourself. My Wellpreneur Marketing Bootcamp is an example of an Online Course.

An Online Course is simply a program, class, workshop or course that's taught online.

It can include written lessons, guides, and worksheets along with audio and video. Online Courses often include access to a protected website which hosts the course materials. Sometimes they include interactive elements like groups or forums, or live calls.

Online Courses can also be delivered Live or Evergreen:

- A Live course means it starts and ends at a specific time, and a group of students go through the course together.

- An Evergreen course means the course content is always available, and a student works through the material at her own pace.

You can create an online course about almost anything. You can teach yoga or fitness, cooking, healthy shopping, meditation, self-care, making DIY skincare... anything you might teach during an in-person workshop you can teach online.

Online Courses are a gold standard in teaching online... but I don't recommend them for a first product because they're a big investment of time and effort to create. You want to be sure you're creating exactly what your target market wants, before you develop an online course.

5. Membership / Subscriptions

From monthly subscription boxes of beauty products, to a monthly emotional eating support group to a weekly subscription of healthy recipes to daily fresh workouts, membership and subscription products are really popular! Unlike an Online Course which is purchased once, a membership is a recurring revenue stream — you get paid every month for as long as a client is a member. Recurring revenue is more predictable, and makes membership products an appealing option to add to your business.

A membership or subscription can be structured however you want. You might deliver a physical or digital product at regular intervals (a box a month, or a new class every week). A membership often includes access to a membership site or private forum just for members. And it often includes a live element (like a group or forum) to connect and get feedback. You might also provide members-only resources or training. You'll just want to be sure your target audience *wants* what you're offering, before you commit to provide it on a recurring basis!

Digital Product Reality Check

Now, if you're thinking: "I know what I'll do! I'll create an online course that people will buy through my website 24/7, so I never have to work with a 1:1 client again!" — let's do a bit of a reality check.

Digital products and courses are often referred to as "evergreen", since they can be always available and require no extra work on your part to *deliver*. These types of digital products are often considered "passive income" (vs, "active" income like a live course or coaching), and seem to be the Holy Grail of digital products.

My Wellpreneur Marketing Bootcamp is an evergreen course like this. But is it completely passive? No way! What the "passive income" evangelists often fail to mention is the active work that goes into marketing and selling the course. Over time, you can optimize paid advertising to find new prospects and then put them in an automated sales funnel to nurture and sell them on the course. That's really smart business once it's setup and optimized, and a great goal to aim for when creating your course. But the reality is that the first course you create won't be your best work, and it won't be totally passive (at least, not if you want to make consistent, or growing, sales).

Don't get caught up in comparison-itis looking at amazing online courses which have been created by experienced entrepreneurs with an entire team to help them, either. As a new wellpreneur, you have the advantage of being able to start small, iterate, and improve each time. You don't need to create The Ultimate Product on your first attempt (and I don't believe you could do this even if you tried). That's not to say your first product won't sell or that won't solve your customer's problems — it can and will — but it won't be anywhere near as good as the products you'll create a year or two from now. It's more important to get something out into the world, get feedback from actual customers, and then improve it.

The fastest way to get to a great (and then amazing) digital product is by starting small, getting it into the hands of customers, and iterating.

ACTION STEP:

- Brainstorm digital product ideas that could solve the problem you identified in the previous step. Don't worry about HOW to create the products yet, just let yourself brainstorm and free-write what some of these products could look like.

Wellpreneur Interview: Alexx Stuart

Alexx Stuart is the creator of Low Tox Life, where she inspires people to do great things for themselves and the planet. In this interview, she shares how she decided to create an Online Course business instead of offering individual services like coaching. Learn more about Alexx at LowToxLife. com.

A couple of years ago I worked with a business coach, and she asked me for my five core values. One of those values was changing the world, and it's a fire I've had in my belly since I was 16 years old. I've always had an activist gene, and I feel you can't be an activist and only help one person. It's just too frustrating. I wanted to reach thousands of people.

I knew I had to do something "one-to-many" as opposed to "one-on-one". So that was how I created an e-course business. So far, I've been able to help 2,500 people in just over 12 months, and it feels fantastic.

To create my first online course, I asked how I could best serve my community at that time. I listened to what they were telling me about their questions and problems. And the question I heard the most was how to find natural products for themselves and their families. They were asking about natural cleaning products, shampoos, face creams etc. So I realized I needed to create a product for beginners, so they could get those basic answers, while the rest of the community kept moving forward as well. I wanted to create a product serving those people at the very beginnings of their journey who needed help reducing toxins in their lives.

Amanda Cook

For me, it's always been about being obsessed with serving the people who are right in front of you.

So often we tell ourselves it's not enough to have 50 Facebook followers. That you can't become successful until you have 5,000 or 50,000. But you'll never get to those bigger numbers if you're not helping the 50 who are in front of you right now. Help them, and they'll tell their friends, and slowly your community will grow.

Listen to the complete interview in the Book Bonuses:
WellpreneurBook.com/bonus

Chapter 5

The Organic Growth System

"Happiness is not something you postpone for the future; it is something you design for the present."

– Jim Rohn

Have you ever wondered how people *actually* make money through their website?

It's all well and good to create an eBook... but how do you actually get people to visit your website? And then get them to take out their credit card and *buy something*? When you're first starting out and only have 10 website visitors a day, including yourself, it can feel impossible!

Online business owners aren't very transparent about how their businesses *actually* work. I worked nights and weekends on my natural beauty blog for two years taking massive action... and did not make a cent. None. Nada. Zip.

I hadn't started a business... just an all-consuming hobby!

Amanda Cook

It turns out I'd made two fundamental mistakes:

1) I was focused on what I wanted to do, not what my audience wanted, and

2) I didn't have a strategy. My approach was just "try everything and something is bound to work!"

I didn't have a strategy because no one was talking about the big picture, they were just teaching piecemeal marketing tactics.

I knew how to grow my email list, but I couldn't see how to turn those subscribers into paying clients. I was building an audience on my Facebook page, but didn't have anything to sell them.

In this chapter, you're going to learn how an online business really works. You'll understand how to bring the right people to your website, and turn them into paying clients.

Once you understand this system, you'll be able to generate revenue faster, and you'll also feel confident about where to focus your time. When you're tempted to start a YouTube channel because the latest internet marketing guru is talking about how it's an essential part of growing your business, you can put it in context of your overall marketing plan. Do you need another content channel? Maybe what you really need is to do more promotion of your existing blog posts to reach a bigger audience. Or maybe you need to stop focusing on growing your list, and instead nurture the subscribers you already have to get more clients. Don't worry if you aren't sure what this means yet — it will all be clear when you understand the Organic Growth System.

Introducing: The Organic Growth System

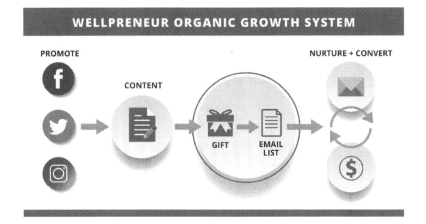

Website visitors become paying clients by flowing through this system from left to right. But to explain how the Organic Growth System works, let's reverse-engineer the system by starting from the center...

Email List

The core of your online wellness business is your email list.

We'll explore this in depth in the next chapter, but having an email list **gives YOU the power to contact your audience**. Rather than posting on your website and *hoping* people will come back to read it, having an email list means you can proactively reach your audience wherever they are, whenever you want to.

(Just to be super clear, we are not talking about scammy, icky, spammy email marketing. As an ethical wellpreneur, you're only going to email people who have voluntarily opted-in to your email list and given you permission to contact them — people who want to hear from you!

Not only is this the right thing to do, but it also means the people you're emailing know you and are therefore more likely to read your emails and take action!)

Opt-In Offer

So how do you get people on your email list? With a valuable free offer. You've probably seen (and signed up for) these types of offers yourself. Your free offer will usually be a digital product like an eBook, mini-course, challenge, video series, guided meditation, toolkit etc. The key is that your free offer has to actually be valuable for your ideal customer.

So your free opt-in offer incentivizes people to join your email list. But how do they find out you even have a free opt-in offer?

Content

This step is why you hear so much about writing blogs and creating videos as a way to build your business. Content is the valuable, expert information you're providing to your audience. It can take many forms based on your strengths and interests. The most common are writing (blogging), video (vlogs or online video) and audio (podcasts.) Potential customers find your content, and then somewhere around that content (either at the end or beside your content) they see your free offer. If they like your content and find it valuable, there's a good chance they'll take you up on your free offer — and voilà! A new email subscriber!

Let's check in. Does that flow make sense so far? Look at the Organic Growth System diagram and follow it through the central steps: Offer relevant, valuable content where your ideal customers can find it, and then make an enticing free offer. A visitor takes your free offer in exchange for joining your email list. And now you have a new subscriber (and potential customer).

Promotion

Once you have interesting, useful content to share, how will your ideal customers find it? This is the Promotion step. There are an endless amount of ways to promote your content to your audience. Here are just a few to get you thinking...

- Tweet it
- Instagram
- Pin it on Pinterest
- Write a Facebook post
- Run Facebook ads
- Do a live streaming video about it (like Facebook Live)
- Write a guest post on a popular blog
- Buy Google Ads
- Appear in Google search results
- Talk about it in media interviews
- Mention it in your workshops
- Get other websites to link to you on their resources page
- Post in forums
- Post in the comments on other blogs
- Put a link in your email footer

The Promotion step is where social media fits into your wellness business marketing plan. It's a platform for building relationships with your community and promoting your content. Rather than selling on social media, why not just get people to share your content, and they'll opt-into your list organically? You can sell to them via your email list later.

Let's review the flow again: you're promoting your valuable content, where people then learn about your free offer, and then join your email list.

The steps we've covered so far will grow your email list steadily and organically. But when do the sales happen? That comes next.

Nurture

Let's jump to the other side of the diagram. Once a new subscriber joins your list, they enter into a 'nurture sequence'. This is the process of building a relationship with that person, so when they're ready (or you're ready) they can buy from you.

Think about your own experience shopping online. Sometimes you go online with the intention of buying (for example, if you're searching for a specific book, or if you have an urgent problem that needs to be solved). But other times, you're just looking for information. You know you have a problem, or you're interested in a topic, but you're not looking to buy anything yet — you're just seeking information or entertainment.

The purpose of an email nurture sequence is to transition subscribers from just being interested, to being ready to buy — and being ready to buy from *you*.

In its simplest form, your nurture sequence can be your regular email newsletter. Every week or month when you send your newsletter, your subscriber is reminded of you, your useful information and the services you provide. If you remain a consistent, valuable presence in their lives through your thoughtful email contact, then when they're ready to buy, they'll think of you first. This is why regular email contact is so important — and why only emailing when you have something to sell doesn't work. You have to build up your relationship (often called the "know, like and trust factor") with your prospective client, so that when they're ready to buy, they'll buy from you.

Most wellpreneurs start with an email newsletter to nurture their subscribers. But as you evolve your online marketing, you'll probably want to create an automated series of emails (called an *email autoresponder*) to move people from new subscriber to paying customer. Most email autoresponders are 'evergreen', meaning that no matter when someone signs up, they'll get the same sequence of emails, and it will always feel fresh and relevant. We'll talk about email nurturing and autoresponders more in Chapter 10: Nurture and Convert.

Convert

Throughout the nurturing (emailing) process, you'll occasionally make offers to your subscribers. How you do this is totally dependent on how you want to run your business. Do you always have products for sale, or are they only available a couple of times per year? Are you fully booked or available to take new clients? Do you offer free taster sessions, or do they always have to pay to get time with you? Are your products and services entry level or premium?

A common scenario is that you might make a special one-time only offer for new subscribers as soon as they sign up, and then you might make another offer for a free session a couple of emails later (to expand on what they learned in your opt-in gift). Many wellpreneurs who sell coaching services put an offer for a taster session in every email newsletter. If you want to launch or re-launch a product or service, you'll often send a series of emails with a special time-limited offer only available during the launch.

The essential idea here is that if you've built a relationship with your list, then you can make periodic offers to get new customers.

That's it — that's the flow from bringing the right people to your website, and turning them into paying clients.

Do you see how the steps work together?

Go back and run through the diagram again, this time from left to right. Look at the flow from initial clicks (from promotion, to your content, to your free offer) to when people become clients (via offers in your email list.)

I cannot emphasize how important it is for you to understand what this flow looks like in your own business. This system explains WHY you would do a guest post or social media (promotion), or why you'd create a free eBook (opt-in) or why your email newsletter is so important (nurturing and conversions).

Once you understand the flow from website visitor to paying client in your business, making decisions becomes easier. You understand exactly how you're going to get clients and make money in your business. You can make better decisions about what marketing activities to do. You can quickly identify where you need to improve the system to make more sales, by working through the Organic Growth System from left to right. And you'll be less overwhelmed, because by focusing on setting up one complete path through the system first, you'll be on the fastest track to generating revenue through your website.

In the coming chapters, we're going to dive into each step of the Organic Growth System, so you'll know exactly how to set it up, as well as tips and tricks to get it working as effectively as possible. I'll also share my own workflow and productivity tips to get the system set up in your own business with minimal frustration.

ACTION STEPS:

- If you'd prefer to listen to me explain this system, listen to the Organic Growth System audio available in the Book Bonuses at WellpreneurBook.com/bonus

- Talk through the Organic Growth System. Can you explain how website visitors turn into paying clients step-by-step?

- Now walk through the Organic Growth System diagram for your business and ask these questions:
    - Which parts exist already, if any?
    - Which parts exist but need to be improved?
    - Which parts don't exist yet?

- You'll find a printable version of the Organic Growth System in the Book Bonuses — you can fill it out for your business and indicate areas you need to create or improve.

Amanda Cook

Wellpreneur Interview: Mark Sisson

Mark Sisson is the bestselling author of The Primal Blueprint and one of the leading voices of the growing Evolutionary Health Movement. Learn more about Mark at MarksDailyApple.com.

You know, I tell my kids I didn't know what I wanted to be until I was 47. I bounced around in a lot of jobs, I worked for other people, I worked for myself, and it wasn't until I was about 47 that I I found the path that led to the kind of success that I envisioned for myself.

I wouldn't change anything about how I got there because it finally hit me at a later age in life, that everything I've done had led me to that point. So, it was all really visceral. It felt so right when it finally hit and I said, "Yes, now I can see doing this for the rest of my life."

When I first started blogging in 2006, I had some grandiose assumptions that within a year I'd have one hundred thousand visitors a day. Well, at the end of one year, I had one thousand visitors a day. So, my high expectations were sorely mismet and yet a lot of people said, "Wow, that's cool. You have a thousand visitors a day. How did you do that?" You have to allow for some amount of growth and some amount of not meeting your expectations, but still being passionate about it.

That's why I didn't quit, because I still loved what I was doing. I knew that if I kept doing it, it would grow to the point that I could begin to monetize it. But that point only happened two and a half to three years after I started the blog.

In retrospect, I'd say be careful about how much you worry, and stress, and sweat and angst over small things. Because ultimately, it'll all work out. And you know, when I look back I can't believe how down I was at times about my life, how I thought I wasn't where I should be based on the expectations I'd set for myself. It was unnecessarily depressing because at the time I still had a nice life. I paid my bills, I didn't go into debt, I had good relationships. All the basic elements of the life I have today, I had then. I just didn't have as much stuff, but that really doesn't matter. So, if I could go back, I'd just tell myself to enjoy the moment and the process more.

Take the time to appreciate what you've done up to this point and then acknowledge going forward. The intention is not to be in agony, and stressed, and worried about all the things that used to keep me up at night, but to enjoy the process and recognize the choice you've made is a good one and that people will benefit from what you're doing.

One of the greatest sources of income for me now is what I call psychic income. If I walk through an airport and somebody comes and, "Oh my god, can I hug you? You saved my life. I've lost a hundred pounds, I'm off my meds. My doctor said I was headed down this slippery-slope." That is huge to me, to be able to get that kind of acknowledgement and realize that something that I did, sitting at my desk, 2,000 miles away from this person, helped transform that person and brought a smile to that person's face. Big stuff.

Listen to the complete interview in the Book Bonuses:
WellpreneurBook.com/bonus

Chapter 6

Your Email List

"The way to get started is to quit talking and begin doing."

– Walt Disney

Now it's time to set up the Organic Growth System in your own business. We're going to start with the core system: setting up your email list.

Setting up an email list for your business is quick, inexpensive, and builds an audience of potential customers, which is incredibly important when you're ready to start selling.

Your email list is at the center of your online wellness business, and puts you in control of your marketing. But with power comes responsibility. Each of these people on your email list has given you permission to contact them about your topic. They're trusting that you're going to keep their email address safe, and that you'll send them useful, relevant information (and occasional offers) that will help them solve their problems or inspire them to reach their goals. If you can automate your email list growth (through the process I'll teach you in this book), then you will have a constant stream of new potential customers.

Why Do I Want an Email List Anyway?

Think of a time when you found a new blog or website that you loved. How did you make sure that you wouldn't forget about it? Maybe you bookmarked it, or followed it on social media. Or maybe you signed up for their email list.

If you're anything like me, your web browser bookmarks might be hundreds of items long, and you rarely (if ever) revisit them. And with social media algorithms changing so quickly, there's no guarantee you'll see updates from the blogs and brands that you like. When it's your business in question, you don't want to rely on other people or platforms to be able to reach your potential customers when you have something to say!

With an email list, YOU have the power to contact your customers. Rather than waiting for them to remember you, you can show up in their inbox, where they are every day (probably multiple times per day). You're going where they already are. And even better, they have invited you to be there, because they believe you can add value to their lives. This is a privilege not to be taken lightly, and it's the key to building your online wellness business.

So, you know you need an email list — how are you going to create one?

If you're just starting out, you might be tempted to DIY your email list with a spreadsheet or in your personal email account because you're on a tight budget or don't want to learn a new tool. This is a huge mistake. Do NOT DIY your email list.

Normally, DIY is awesome. But your email list is not the place to try to do-it-yourself, even if you're a beginner with a limited budget. Here's why:

Four Reasons NOT to DIY Your Email List

1. Professionalism. You're creating this email list as part of your business. You need to build credibility and authority with your audience, so they'll feel confident buying from you. Sending professional looking emails is part of this overall approach. Even if you're just starting out, shift into a business mindset, and start acting like the business you'll become, rather than the solopreneur you are today.

2. Deliverability. When you email your customers, you want to make sure that it actually reaches them. Email marketing services have systems in place to improve deliverability, so your mail goes into the inbox, and not into the spam filter. If you start sending bulk emails from your personal account, some people might start flagging you as a spammer, and then no one will get your emails — business or personal!

3. Anti-spam laws and administrative headaches. No one likes spam. It has become such a huge problem that the US, Canada, the EU and several other countries have passed anti-spam laws. The details are different in each location, but two key points are that you should only email people who have voluntarily joined your list, and you need to offer an easy way to unsubscribe. Email marketing services do both of these for you. With an email service, a person must confirm that they want to join your list, and on each email, there is a simple 'unsubscribe me' button. Each country has different laws for email marketing, so make sure you check your local laws before sending.

4. Automation. Email marketing services are designed to manage email lists. They make routine tasks like subscribes and unsubscribes easy and automatic. Most services have pre-designed templates you can use to make a professional looking email. You can also copy previous newsletters to have a consistent look and feel every month. Many services also provide statistics about how many people read your emails, and which links were clicked. It would take you hours to manage all of this on your own!

So instead of DIY, you want to use an Email Marketing Service to contact your subscribers.

Choosing an Email Marketing Service

The major decision in setting up your email list is choosing which Email Marketing Service to use.

Here are the features you want to look for in an Email Marketing Service:

- Complies with your country's anti-spam laws

- Automatic de-duplication so each email address only appears once in your list (so that people don't get multiple copies of the same email)

- Enables 'one click unsubscribe' (so people can easily leave your list)

- Ability to export your list (in case you want to move to a new provider)

- Ability to import new subscribers (in case you get manual signups at a workshop or event)

- Autoresponder or automated email sequence capability

- Mobile responsive emails (so people can easily read your mail from a mobile device)

- Metrics and analytics (number of opens, clicks, unsubscribes)

- Ability to 'group' or 'tag' subscribers into categories within a list (so you can contact subsets of your list for different interest areas.)

There are many Email Marketing Services, and this industry changes quickly, so you can find my current recommendations in the Book Bonuses.

How an Email Marketing Service Works

It will be easier to set up your own email list if you understand how the process works from a technical perspective.

Your **email list** is the actual location where your email addresses are stored. You can think of this as a massive database or spreadsheet, or simply as a list of people's email addresses. At a minimum, each person on your list is identified by an email address. You might also choose to store other information about them as well. For example, on my list I capture the first name and the email address. I use the first name to personalize the emails I send. I used to capture the last name as well, but realized I hardly ever used it (when someone makes a purchase from me, they enter their full name at that point, so I don't need it in the email list before they're a customer).

A **signup form** is the actual form where people type in their email address and first name, and then click a 'submit' button to join your list. You've surely used some of these yourself in the past, for example to download an eBook or join an email newsletter. As an example, when you go to the Book Bonuses page for the first time, you'll see a signup form asking you to register to get access to the bonuses.

The signup forms will appear on your website, on a landing page (a dedicated webpage only for email signups), and possibly on social media.

The process works like this: a person sees one of your signup forms and decides to take your offer (for a newsletter or a free gift etc.). They enter their email address (and possibly first name) and click 'submit'.

What happens next depends on whether you've set your list for 'single opt-in' or 'double opt-in'.

With single opt-in, when a person clicks the submit button, she is automatically added to your email list, and typically a free gift is delivered (either in an email, or on a 'thank you' webpage)

With double opt-in, the subscriber has to take one final step. When the person enters her name and email address and clicks submit, she's redirected to a page that says something like *"One more step! You need to check your email and click the link to be added to my email list."* The email system then sends an automatic email to her with a link inside.

She must open the email and click the link, and THEN she will be added to the list and sent the free gift.

Why the extra step? The idea behind the double opt-in is to prevent spammy signups. Theoretically, with a single opt-in, you could subscribe ANY email address to your mailing list. You could sign up your friend, or your coworker, or your mother, or someone you dislike, or a total stranger. A double opt-in confirmation ensures that only the email address owner is able to add themselves to the list, because they have to click a link in an email before they're confirmed on the list.

So with a single opt-in list you'll typically get more subscribers, but they might be less engaged (because they might not have signed themselves up). With a double opt-in you'll get fewer subscribers but you know they want to hear from you!

Two Final Points When Setting Up Your Email List

Although the details to set up your email marketing will differ for each tool, here are two points you don't want to miss:

1. Physical Address. To comply with US anti-spam laws, you'll be asked for a physical business address when you setup your email list. *This address will appear on the bottom of every email you send!* Let me repeat that — whatever mailing address you enter, will be public knowledge to anyone on your email list, as it will appear on the bottom of each email!

This is a personal decision, but I would never put my home address on my email list. Safety first — you don't know who is going to subscribe to your list, so don't take the risk. The best choice is to use a business address if you have one. If you don't have a business address, you can rent a PO Box or purchase a mail forwarding service which provides a separate mailing address. Of course, anti-spam laws change, so read the updated guidance from your email provider. Remember that each country has different email marketing laws, so make sure to check out your local regulations before sending.

2. Unsubscribe/Subscribe notifications. Many email providers give you the option to be notified when a new subscribers joins or leaves your email list. This is really tempting in the beginning because you're focused on growing your list, and you want to stay on top of new subscribers. From experience, I recommend NOT enabling these notifications. Receiving subscribe/unsubscribe notifications puts you on an emotional roller coaster that is completely distracting from your real work. I received these notifications for the first year I had my blog, and it was awful. When I got new subscribers, I was so excited! But a single unsubscriber would make me feel like a failure. I would go into the spiral of despair (you know the one I'm talking about), so learn from my mistake and stop the crazy before it starts. Do not get notifications for subscribes or unsubscribes. You can log into your email system once a week and check the metrics — you don't need to see it as it happens.

And unsubscribes happen. It doesn't mean people don't like you, or that you're doing a 'bad job' (whatever that means). People just unsubscribe. Haven't you gone through times where you decide to unsubscribe from all your email newsletters? It doesn't mean you don't like the person, it's just that you're decluttering your inbox, or your needs have changed, you just aren't reading them — it's fine, it happens, and as as your email list grows you will get unsubscribes *every single time your send an email.* Every time! It's just part of having an email list. It's no big deal. The goal is to have your subscriptions automated so your list is always growing, and then the unsubscribes don't matter. Anyway, you only want people on your list who WANT to be there, so let people unsubscribe and go on their way if they don't want to work with you. There are enough subscribers and customers who do want to hear from you to keep yourself busy!

ACTION STEPS:

- Choose an email list provider (see the Book Bonuses for my latest recommendations)

- Create your email list

- Test your email list (sign up for your list yourself, and test how the process works)

Amanda Cook

Wellpreneur Expert Interview: Nathan Barry

In this interview Nathan Barry, the founder of email marketing service ConvertKit, shares how to get your first email subscribers. Learn more about Nathan at NathanBarry.com.

When you're just getting started and have no or very few subscribers, you need to follow something called the 10-person rule.

Step 1 is to figure out your topic. Hopefully, you know that. Narrow it down, get it to be pretty specific. I'll use my topic as an example — I taught people how to design iPhone applications.

Step 2 is to list out 10 people you know personally who want to learn what you're teaching. So, I listed out my programmer friends who wanted to learn design, and then my beginner techie friends who were just trying to get into it and learn design as well. (If you can't get to ten interested people for your topic, maybe this is not the topic to focus on.) But 10 people should be pretty easy.

Step 3 is to send each of your 10 people a personal email and say, *"Hey, I'm starting a new site, an email list, where I'm talking about [TOPIC]. Is that something you'd be interested in?"* Hopefully, since your list is pretty targeted and you know these people, eight of those people should get back to you and say *"Yes. I'm interested."* There's your first eight email subscribers. They've all given you permission to add you to their email list. Now you have someone to send to!

Step 4 is to email these people again (a personal email, not from an email marketing service), and ask two questions:

1) "What are you struggling with related to this topic? What's your biggest frustration related to learning how to [insert your topic here]?"

2) "Where do you go online right now to learn about [this topic]?"

Take the responses you receive and put them in a spreadsheet. The first question, their biggest frustration, tells you what to write about. Often, in those early days, it can be really hard to know what to write about and what to focus on. So if you just write to answer each person's frustrations, you will help each of your early subscribers, and if it's useful to one, it will be useful to many. That will give you your initial content.

The second question, "Where do you go online right now to learn about this?" will tell you about the Twitter accounts they follow, the websites, the communities. You're basically getting your friends to do your research for you and tell you about communities you probably didn't know existed, and that will give you places to share your content, and give you communities and forums you can participate in.

That's the process to get you started.

If that worked with 10 people, just keep doing it. I know a lot of people who have reached their first hundred subscribers or more purely through cold outreach. Just saying, "Hey, thanks for sharing my article. Would you want to join my email list?" Or if you have a friend or a Facebook friend who you think might be interested, just ask them if they'd like to join your email list. That's how you get started.

Listen to the complete interview in the Book Bonuses: WellpreneurBook.com/bonus

Wellpreneur Interview: Sean Croxton

Sean Croxton is the founder of Underground Wellness. In this interview he shares his experiences with email marketing (and unsubscribes!) and his advice to new wellpreneurs. Learn more about Sean at SeanCroxton.com.

I have a list of 80,000 subscribers that acts like a list of 200,000 because it's so responsive. I have a high open rate and an engaged following. But still, I get between 150 and 300 unsubscribes every single time I send out an email! And I don't care. If you unsubscribe, you're not part of my tribe, period. Take your free stuff and go. Because the people who hang on and chill and engage are amazing. So unsubscribes are actually a good thing.

Then once you have that tribe, listen to what they want. If you're just starting online, don't even think about your product yet. You should be thinking about building up your credibility and putting out really good content. Engage with your people on Facebook and Twitter and email, and you'll start seeing those common denominators that lead to a product. I created The Dark Side of Fat Loss program because I heard from people who couldn't afford to work with me and wanted another way to go through the program. So that program is almost word-for-word what I used to say to my clients during sessions. It was quick to create because I'd said it a hundred times before.

Through my work, I talk with a lot of aspiring wellness entrepreneurs. I so often see people who have gone to lots of conferences and taken all the online courses, but haven't posted their first blog yet (or video, or podcast). It's just so hard for them to get started. They have fears around rejection and judgment and the the big changes that may happen in their life.

But you have to start. If you're somebody out there who is taking 8 million different courses and you haven't done anything yet, stop taking courses. Start your blog. You don't even have to have a website. When I first started my YouTube channel, I didn't have a website, I used MySpace! So you can even just send people to your Facebook page.

Get people onto an email list and just start. There are people out there who are looking for you. And they're not going to find you if you haven't started. They're not going to be helped or served by you until you put your content out. So just start.

Listen to the complete interview in the Book Bonuses:
WellpreneurBook.com/bonus

Chapter 7

Your Email Opt-In Gift

"When I chased after money, I never had enough. When I got my life on purpose and focused on giving of myself and everything that arrived into my life, then I was prosperous."

- Dr. Wayne Dyer

Now that you've setup your email list, it's time to find your first subscribers.

Most new email list owners put a big box on their website: "Subscribe to my newsletter!" But honestly: who wants to get another email newsletter?

That offer is not compelling. Visitors will think, "What's in it for me? Are you just going to mail me every week trying to sell me stuff? How often are you going to contact me? Is there going to be anything valuable in it, or just a sales pitch?" When an offer raises more questions than it answers, your potential customers will just walk away (safer to protect their email inbox than to take a chance on this unknown person, even if they did enjoy your recent blog post).

You can do much better than this. Using the following strategy, you'll not only get people eager to sign up for your email list, but they'll be the *right* people (the ones who are most likely to turn into potential customers).

Let's remember the goal of your email opt-in gift:

- Get people to join your email list (a value exchange)

- Demonstrate that you can help with their specific problem (expertise)

- Start to build a relationship with the customer (know, like and trust factor)

- Set the tone and expectations for your brand and business (are you playful? Serious? Sarcastic? Holistic? Warm? Chatty? Clinical?)

- Invite them to take the next step with you (perhaps doing a free clarity session with you, or buying an entry-level product.)

The best free opt-in gifts are relevant to the target audience and problem, easy to consume, help the subscriber get a specific result, and engage the subscriber with you over a period of time.

 Your first opt-in gift doesn't need to be perfect, and doesn't need to solve all of your potential client's problems. It's the first of many opt-in gifts you'll create in your business. Just follow the steps and keep moving forward!

It's tempting to want to create the Best Opt-In Gift Ever which will skyrocket your list into the thousands overnight! But when you put so much pressure on yourself to make a "perfect" opt-in gift, usually one of these three things happens:

- You get paralyzed and don't take any action. As a placeholder, you just put a 'Sign up for my email newsletter' box on your website and wonder why people aren't signing up.

- You want to attract as many people as possible, so you create a generic PDF download like 'three green smoothie recipes'. No one signs up, because that's too generic, and you can get about a million green smoothie recipes just by Googling it.

- You're determined to make the 'perfect' opt-in gift and get stuck on this step for months, writing the best eBook ever which encapsulates your entire system, loads of recipes, and is professionally laid out. Meanwhile, your email list isn't growing and you're not finding clients because no one has seen your opt-in gift yet!

Mindset Shift: What if creating an opt-in gift didn't have to be so hard? What if it was easy?

After all, this isn't your only opt-in gift, it's the first of many!

This first opt-in gift is simply moving your Six-Month Target Market customer a bit further along on her journey to solve a piece of her problem.

It doesn't have to solve all of her problems, or the entire problem, or appeal to everyone, or be a defining product in your business. You're just providing value for this one specific person on this one specific problem... and later down the road as you expand your business you'll create additional opt-ins which can target different people, different problems or lead to different products and services. Remember, we want to create one complete path from opt-in to client!

Free vs. Paid

How much value and information should you give away for free? "If I give away too much, why would they ever hire me? Shouldn't I keep my best information and tips only for paying clients?" These are really common questions among new wellpreneurs.

I understand this concern, because it *seems* like you should only give your best work to your paying clients.

The challenge is that you have to work harder to build a relationship with someone online.

So if you only give away semi-useful, fluffy information for free — why would anyone trust you enough to pay you? You've got to demonstrate your expertise and build your know/like/trust factor by giving away good, quality information and tips that people can use to get results.

There is a balance here though. While you do want to give away valuable, useful, actionable information... **you don't need to give away your entire system.**

And not because it's too valuable to give away! The real reason you don't want to give away your entire system at once, is because when you give everything you've got in one shot, it's totally overwhelming -- and your potential customers won't benefit from that.

Just imagine that you put *everything* you know about health and wellness and healthy living into an eBook. Everything you know on how to solve all your client's problems. All of the resources and ideas and strategies and advice about how they can transform their lives, from beginner through to advanced level.

Most likely, the reader would be totally overwhelmed. Where would she even start? She's a beginner. It would be way too much information to be able to take action on, and she'd just put it aside and never see results.

And more importantly, even if you could provide all of the information to solve her complete problem — would she actually do it? Probably not. Because the reality is that **people don't need *more* information, they need the information they already have broken down into bite-sized chunks, and the support to implement it into their lives.**

For most people, a book alone is not the complete solution.

But imagine a super motivated client DID take action and solve her problem using your information. Wouldn't that still create additional areas for your support? Now that she's on the path to transformation, how will she maintain the results? Where will she get support and advice on the new lifestyle that results from the change? How might that change impact her relationships/job/clothing/budget? And if you did solve this one problem that had such a massive impact on her life, she would likely be so enthusiastic that she'd be even more ready to pay to work with you (if your free information is that good — just imagine how good the paid stuff is)!

Giving away too much is not a problem you need to worry about.

Most people need support and help to implement a solution to their problem, and that's something you can't offer in a free product.

It's more important that your opt-in makes it as easy as possible for your new visitor to access your material, take action on it, and see some results (and get to know, like and trust you in the process). Then you can show her what the next step is in going further and getting more support, information and results by working with you.

Create Your Opt-In Gift

In this chapter, you're going to create an opt-in gift that solves one specific tiny part of the main problem you've identified. You want to give your potential client just enough information that they can take action, see some results, find it useful, realize that you know what you're talking about, and leave them wanting more. Remember, your goal isn't to have the biggest email list, it's to have a *targeted* email list, filled with people who are ideal potential clients.

Four steps to creating your opt-in gift:

1. **A Little Slice**

2. **Define the Title and Benefits**

3. **Create the Opt-In**

4. **Deliver the Opt-In**

Step 1: A Little Slice

Your opt-in is going to solve one part of your main problem for your target audience. It should be appealing and valuable specifically for them — not for everyone in the world. We don't want everyone to sign up for our email list, we just want our ideal clients to join, so let's make the opt-in work for them.

Imagine that you have a big, delicious, double-layered cake. The cake represents all the good stuff that clients hope to achieve by working with you — the solutions to their problems and the benefits to their life. Your clients want that cake. So in your opt-in gift, we don't want to give them the whole cake (and you couldn't anyway, as we discussed earlier), we just want to give them a little slice. A single slice of cake that solves or improves one problem and gives them some good results, so that they think "Wow, if this free slice of cake was so good, just imagine if I bought the entire cake!"

There are lots of slices in a cake. Lots of options for what you could solve in your opt-in gift. I suggest picking a problem that is "top of mind" for your client (something she might search on Google or buy a book about), and something that you can help her solve with a free opt-in gift. It's also good if you can solve or improve the problem immediately, or quickly (within a week) after taking action on your opt-in gift. So choose something small.

For example, if you're a health coach specializing in holistic skin care, and your primary paid service is a three or six month coaching package, perhaps you could offer a free five-day 'detox' or 'reboot' or 'jump start' to help clients start to clear up their skin on their own. Or if one of their concerns was how to know what beauty products won't irritate their skin, perhaps you could write an eBook or resources list with the best natural skincare products to make or buy for women with sensitive skin.

If you're targeting weight loss for men as your main problem, you could do something similar — you could either create a short (three to seven day) 'challenge' or 'detox' or 'reboot' (whatever language works for your audience) to help them start changing their lifestyles and experiencing results. Or you could create a guide or resource list answering one of their main questions — like where to order these healthy ingredients, or a video series with your favorite 10-minute exercise routine for days they're too busy, or a three-day meal plan with recipes.

Don't overcomplicate this, and don't worry too much about the format yet. Just identify a little slice of the problem that you could solve, that would be valuable to your target customer. And don't worry about giving too much value. When in doubt, give MORE value, not less.

Exercise: A Little Slice

Here's a brainstorming exercise you can use to identify possible topics for your opt-in gift. Take a sheet of paper and write your Six-Month Target Market statement at the top: "I help <target market> to <main problem>."

Set a timer for 10 minutes. Then just brainstorm all the little problems and ideas that go along with that main problem.

So if your customer is new moms, and the problem is that they want to get back to their pre-baby weight, you might have a list like this:

- I don't know what to eat

- I'm too busy to exercise

- I don't want to cook different food for me and the family

- I don't know where to buy these healthy ingredients

- I'm not sure what exercises are most effective

- I'm not sure how fast I can lose weight realistically

- I'm worried that not sleeping well is affecting my weight loss

- How does breastfeeding affect my weight loss?

- I don't know how often I need to exercise

- I just want someone to tell me exactly what to do

Write down everything that comes to mind, at least 15 problems or questions around your main problem.

Then step away and have some tea, get outside, exercise, anything to clear your brain and get perspective

Then come back to the list. Which of these mini-problems does your ideal customer think is disrupting her life the most or causing the biggest negative impact? (Remember it's important to choose the mini-problem that *your ideal customer thinks* is the problem... not the root cause you've identified as the expert!)

Choose the one with the biggest impact that you can improve or resolve through your opt-in gift.

If you still can't decide, revisit your market research interviews or actually ask someone from that market which mini-problem would be most useful or appealing for her to solve.

For example, from the list above you could create a one-week exercise plan (with or without videos) for new moms. Or a one-week meal planner. Or an eBook about weight loss for new moms who aren't breastfeeding. Or a five-day jump-start program telling them what to eat and how to exercise for five days. Or an eBook with tips on weight loss for new moms who don't have any time and aren't sleeping. There are any number of ideas, but the point is that you can find many ways to solve a slice of their main problem — so just pick the one that's most appealing to them!

Step 2: Define the Title and Benefits

You've got the piece of the problem you're going to solve with your opt-in. But don't start writing just yet! You'll save lots of time and produce a more focused, valuable opt-in if you first identify the specific benefits your potential customer is going to get from this gift.

An enticing title and clear, compelling benefit bullet points are what makes the difference between a magnetic and irresistible opt-in, and an eBook that never gets read. You could create the most informative, practical, gorgeous, professional eBook, but unless you can clearly state why your potential customer should read your book, you won't get any subscribers.

The first step is to create a working title. You don't need to get the final title right now — but brainstorm a list of six to eight potential titles for your free opt-in gift. Write them down. Writing effective titles is a copywriting skill that's beyond the scope of this book, but visit the Book Bonuses for my favorite copywriting resources.

Next, write a list of benefits bullet points. Remember to think like your customer, and use her exact words in these bullets (directly from your market research!) What's in it for her? What should she download your free gift? Brainstorm at least 10 potential benefits bullets, and then select the top three to use in your marketing.

For example, you might have "The 10 best natural beauty products for problem skin (and how to use them!)" as a working title, and the benefits bullets are:

- Discover the key ingredients to avoid that lead to breakouts!

- Learn my top 10 favorite natural beauty products that help your skin heal

- Find the exact order and technique to use your products for clearer skin

If you're not sure which to pick, you can always ask your market research participants which title is most appealing to them. But don't get stuck here. Just pick the best option you have so far and move forward.

Write down your working title and benefits bullets, and keep them nearby while you're creating your opt-in, so you stay focused on the big picture and delivering the right value!

Step 3: Create the Opt-In

Now it's the moment you've been waiting for you — to actually start creating your amazing opt-in gift!

Here's how you'll create your opt-in gift.

1. Choose the format (eBook or PDF, video, audio, e-course, toolkit etc.)

2. Outline what you're going to put in the gift

3. Write, draft and create the content

4. Layout, design and editing

1. First you want to choose the format. You might want to revisit the chapter on digital products if you'd like a refresher on the types of products you could create. Remember, keep it simple!

Pick the format based on your strengths (are you a better writer, or do you love being on video?), what kind of content your ideal customer likes (do they listen to podcasts? Love or hate online video?) and what feels easiest for you to create for this first opt-in gift.

2. Outline the contents of your opt-in gift. Remember that most people are beginners, and don't know how to get started solving this problem. Most opt-ins shouldn't need too much research. You can simply share your process and your best tips in your area of expertise, and most importantly, put them in a simple structure so the reader can take action! Keep it simple. As a free opt-in gift, can you break the solution down into three to seven easy to follow steps? **It's more important you give her *just enough information* that she can**

really take action on to see results, rather than trying to cram in everything you know to 'prove' your expertise!

3. Now it's finally time to create the content. Write the content for the eBook or guide, write the emails, or create the videos or audio. You don't need to use any fancy programs to create the content. Just write it directly in your word processing program or on Google Docs, and don't worry about the layout or formatting at all — you're just creating the content. We'll make it look professional in the next step. Remember to use the exact words and phrases from your market research when you're creating your content! This will build a connection with your customer even quicker, because not only are you solving her problem but you're speaking her language.

I recommend creating your content in one big push, then stepping away for a day or two, and coming back with fresh eyes to edit and revise it.

Once you're happy with the content, it's time to choose the final title and benefits bullet points that you'll use for your opt-in gift.

4. The final step is production — making it look professional. Depending on the format, this might involve creating a PDF yourself or hiring a designer to do it, getting videos or audio edited, or nothing at all if you are doing an e-course and simply sending emails. When you're just starting out with a limited budget, it can feel impossible to get help to make your opt-in look professional. That's why I encourage you to do your content creation first (that's the hardest part), and save the layout for later.

If you want a PDF ebook or guide, you'll need to get your text laid out so it looks professional (you could just 'print to PDF' from your word processing program, but getting a professional cover and layout done will make you feel so much better about the final product!) There are two choices here: you either do the layout yourself, or you hire someone to do it. That's it. Those are your two choices.

If you want to do the layout yourself, I recommend using a simple graphic design program (check the Book Bonuses for my current recommendations) to create a 'Letter' or 'A4' sized document, and then save it as a PDF.

Alternatively, you can hire a designer very inexpensively (or expensively, depending on who you choose) to do the layout for you, and this is the option I recommend for most people. I've recommended websites where you can hire affordable designers in the Book Bonuses.

Don't be shy about asking your entrepreneurial friends or other wellpreneurs for a recommendation for a designer that they've worked with before. When choosing a designer, take a look at their previous work and make sure you like their style. If not, move along and find someone else. You'll also want to provide your logo and color scheme (if you have them), or any guidance about how you want the look and feel of the layout to be. It's your brand and business, so ask for what you want — designers aren't mind readers and you need to be clear about how you want your brand and products to look.

At the end of this step, you'll have your actual opt-in, whether that is a series of emails, a video, or a beautiful PDF document. How exciting! (Getting your first professionally designed PDF guide or eBook back can be one of those 'Oh wow, I'm really a business owner!" moments — enjoy it!)

Step 4: Deliver the Opt-In Gift

Now it's finally time to set up your opt-in so you can start getting new subscribers.

The exact steps to deliver your Opt-In Gift will depend on the tools you use, but here is the basic flow:

First, you'll want to create a list in your Email Marketing Service to automatically deliver the gift when a new subscriber joins. (There should be instructions in the Help area of your Email Marketing Service on how to do this as it's a very common task.)

If your Opt In Gift is a file (like a video file or PDF guide), do NOT include it as an attachment to the email. Instead, you want to upload the file to a cloud service (like Dropbox or Google Drive), and then simply link to your file from the email. When the subscriber clicks the link, they'll be able to download the file directly from the cloud. Alternatively some email marketing providers have their own file hosting capability so you can simply upload your eBook or PDF, and they'll give you a link to use in your email.

Second, you'll want to add a signup form for your new email list to your website. Again, there will be instructions on how to do this in the Help area of your Email Marketing Service.

Third, you'll also want to consider creating a landing page with a signup form as well. A landing page is a dedicated webpage that

ONLY allows people to sign up for your email list. There's no header, no sidebar, no links to your blog posts — this page ONLY presents your opt-in gift (with your compelling title and benefit bullets). The reader is forced to make a decision — will they sign up for your opt-in or not? Presenting them with only one decision on a dedicated landing page like this dramatically increases subscribers to your email list (you should target at least 50% conversion on this page — so half of the people who visit this page will sign up for your free offer). You can find my latest landing page software recommendations in the Book Bonuses.

Finally, test your Opt-In Gift by signing up through one of your signup forms. Does it work like you expected? Do you receive the gift when you sign up? Test it from a computer and a mobile device (you might need to use two different email addresses to do this).

Once you've tested it, you might also ask a friend to test signing up from a different location, just to make 100% sure it's all working correctly. Ask for feedback on the process. Was it easy to to do? Did they understand how to download your eBook etc?

Yes?

Now it's time to celebrate!

Seriously, this is a HUGE milestone and setting up your free opt-in offer is a step that many wellpreneurs put off forever. You're on your way to building your email list of subscribers (and potential customers) for your wellness business! Take a moment to appreciate this big step forward in your business, and feel confident that now you have an automated system to build your online community 24/7.

You now have the core of the Organic Growth System created in your business.

ACTION STEPS:

- Use the exercises in this chapter to decide on your first opt-in gift.

- Create your opt-in gift.

- Test your opt-in gift delivery using your own email address.

- Let us celebrate this milestone with you! (And get you some new subscribers!) Share a link to your opt-in signup page with the hashtag #wellpreneurbook

Wellpreneur Interview: Brett Larkin

Brett Larkin is an online yoga teacher who works with students around the world through her YouTube channel, app and online programs. In this interview she shares her email marketing approach and how her business has developed. Learn more about Brett at BrettLarkin.com.

I'm a little obsessed with email marketing. I have five or six different opt-in gifts on my site that give a ton of value depending on a specific situation. I have one for yoga teachers or aspiring yoga teachers, and one for total yoga beginners. There's one opt-in that's for brides who want to use yoga and mindfulness in their wedding planning, and a more general opt-in on my site which is yoga for abs. So if I don't know anything else about you (like that you're getting married or want to be a yoga teacher), I'll just send you a secret yoga workout that strengthens your core muscles.

I'm a little atypical as a yoga teacher because I don't teach much in studios. I teach yoga online but also meditation, sell courses around yoga and meditation, and also sell physical products like yoga props.

I always had the perspective that teaching yoga full time could never be an option for me, because who really makes money teaching yoga?! But over the past three years my perspective has really shifted. I've realized that online there's a huge opportunity for scale and to make a bigger impact.

It never occurred to me I was starting a business until I realized my YouTube numbers were really good. Once I noticed I was getting a lot of growth and engagement, I started rolling out paid courses and e-commerce.

A big turning point for me was when my channel got big enough that I was invited to go to YouTube and meet other YouTube creators. Before that, I felt like this whole idea of the "six-figure online business" was a myth. I heard people talk about it, but I was very skeptical. But when I went to YouTube, I was surrounded with 300 people all making full-time livings just on YouTube in different niches.

It was so inspiring, and they gave me so much advice. I really want to encourage you to surround yourself with a community. It makes what you're doing feel so much more real and tangible, and they can guide you and show you the way!

Listen to the complete interview in the Book Bonuses: WellpreneurBook.com/bonus

Chapter 8

Your Irresistible Content

"You won't get anything unless you have the vision to imagine it."

– John Lennon

Have you ever been told that you have to blog to grow your business online? Or that blogging is dead, and these days, YouTube videos are the secret to online success? How do you know what's best for your business, and when will you ever find the time on top of doing your *actual work*?!

That's what we're going to tackle in this chapter. By the end of this chapter you'll know exactly what kind of content will attract your ideal client, what kind of content to create, how often to publish, *and* you'll have my proven strategies to make content creation feel easy.

If you've followed along with the Organic Growth System, you understand why and how content fits into your overall marketing plan. Content establishes you as an expert to your target market, and attracts ideal clients to join your email list. It's important to keep this in mind when you're planning content for your business. Your content isn't "extra work" or just a trendy thing to do — it's an essential part of your online business growth strategy.

Content is a general term for the valuable information that you create and share. Content can be written (like a blog), video (like on YouTube) or audio (like a podcast.) It doesn't matter what format of content you produce, what matters is the quality and consistency. The current "hot" content is trend-driven: First it was blogging, then YouTube videos, then podcasting. Right now, everyone wants to do livestream video, and soon enough it will be something else. Formats change, but high quality content never goes out of style. **So don't stress out about what format to create, and instead focus on delivering value.**

What Kind of Content Should I Create?

You can be successful with any type of content. There are examples of wellpreneurs absolutely crushing it and growing huge businesses through blogs, vlogs, or podcasts. So when you're choosing the kind of content you want to produce, consider these three questions:

1. **Your Strengths.** What are your strengths? Are you a better writer or speaker? Do you love being on video, or hate it? What format will let you shine?

2. **Your Ideal Client's Preferences.** What kind of content does your ideal client prefer? Some people love online video. Personally, I hate it. I'll go out of my way not to watch an online video, I'd much rather read. But many people feel the exact opposite — they love watching videos and hate reading. So, what does your ideal client prefer? Where are they when they consume your content? (For example, my wellpreneur podcast listeners love the audio format because they can listen on the go — but many people have never listened to a podcast

and can't imagine when they would, so it all depends on the audience!)

3. **Ease and Consistency.** What can you produce consistently? Sure your video looks amazing when you can borrow a friend's photo studio to film it — but is that realistic for you to produce on a weekly basis? Does it take you hours to write a blog post? Can you really do that every week? There is no right answer here, it's totally up to you and what resources you have available and what fits into your life and business.

 Don't let yourself get stuck here. Remember, in the future you can always expand into other types of content or even hire someone to create it for you! For now, just pick which format feels the most achievable and exciting for you — and let's get started!

How Often Should I Create Content?

Whatever you can do consistently.

Have you ever followed a blog that puts out a flurry of posts at one time, with loads of promotion, and then goes silent for two months? It feels strange, right? Inconsistent publishing raises questions about your focus and professionalism, and certainly doesn't establish credibility with your potential customers. It makes people think you're only publishing when you want them to buy something, which doesn't create a sense of trust.

So if you want to be successful with bringing in new clients through content, you need to choose a frequency you can stick with for the long haul. Content creation is a marathon. You'll be creating content on your topic area on a regular basis for as long as your business exists, so don't burn yourself out at the beginning!

There are two general philosophies of content creation:

The first option is to create content as frequently as possible, maybe once a day (or even multiple times per day!) with the idea that more new content will attract more new readers.

The second philosophy is to *write less and promote more*. With this approach, you produce less content (maybe once per week), but you promote that content everywhere. On social media multiple times, to your email list, possibly with paid advertising — promote, promote, promote! The idea with this approach is that you only have a limited amount of new content, but you're getting it in front of so many new audiences that you attract new readers.

For most wellpreneurs, I recommend the second approach: create less and promote more. I've tried both approaches with my natural beauty website, and found the second was not only more effective, but much more sustainable. When I first started that website, I published a new blog post twice a week, but I felt like I wasn't growing quickly enough. I increased my blogging to three or four times a week. I was writing constantly, but I still felt like it was growing too slowly. It wasn't until I shifted my thinking that I finally grew my email list from 700 to 3,000 subscribers in one year. The reason for that growth had nothing to do with how much I was publishing — instead, I started guest posting on other blogs, not just publishing my own!

When I started writing less content for my own blog and focused on creating content for bigger websites, it put me in front of a large new audience of ideal clients who could join my email list. This strategy is called "guest posting", and if you choose your platforms wisely (so you write for sites that your ideal client is *already reading*) it can be an extremely effective way to grow your audience quickly.

In a nutshell, start with a content creation schedule that feels do-able. Somewhere between once a day and once a month is probably the right frequency. Many people do once per week. If that feels unrealistic, try every two weeks (two per month, or 24 per year). You can always increase the frequency once you get into a rhythm! You can use any extra time to build out your Organic Growth System, promote, write guest posts etc. **Start with a small, achievable goal that you can exceed, rather than setting a hugely ambitious goal and feeling like a failure.**

What Should I Write or Talk About?

It's easy to say you're going to write one blog post per week... and then never do it because you can't decide what to write about.

Here's the key to finding engaging content topics: Your content is not about you!

Let me say that again. Your content, is NOT about YOU. It doesn't really matter what *you* want to write about. What matters is *what your ideal customer is looking for.*

Remember how content fits into your overall strategy: it's attracting new potential clients into your world! In order to attract new potential clients, **you have to create what they're already searching for**. What are they already interested in? What are they Googling? What questions do they have? What are their dreams and desires? That's what you're going to create your content about.

Here's a little exercise I use with my clients plan their content for the next six months.

Exercise: Content Creation

1) Free Flow Brainstorming — set a timer for 10 minutes, and just write down potential ideas for blog posts (or videos or podcasts). Don't censor yourself, just brainstorm. Here are some questions to ask yourself:

- What am I really excited to write about?

- What are the top questions (FAQ's) that people ask me about my subject area?

- What is trendy or current in my industry right now?

- What are the top mistakes that people make in my subject area?

- What do people THINK is good for them in my subject area, but really isn't?

- What do I wish I could go back and tell myself, when I was just learning about my subject area?

- What are my top five tips for people in my subject area?

- What are my top recommended resources (websites, books etc.) in my subject area?

2) Walk away from the list for a few minutes to clear your head. Review your business vision, your ideal client and the problems you can help solve from earlier in this book. Now read through your list of content ideas again, **indicating those topics which either fit with your vision and directly solve your client's problems, or speak to their dreams and desires.**

3) How many ideas do you have highlighted? You might even add some more to your list at this point, specifically in line with your business vision and your ideal client's needs.

4) Review the list again, and pick out the top 10 content ideas. You're going to create these first. You might put them in order of priority, or just pick a top 10, whatever feels best to you.

That's it! If you're going to publish one post per week, those 10 posts will take you through almost three months of content. If you want to do six months, then keep going with the exercise and choose additional topics. In the next step, we'll organize our ideas into an editorial calendar.

Get Organized with an Editorial Calendar

An editorial calendar is a schedule of when you're going to release each piece of content for the next six months. It is a huge timesaver!

The editorial calendar stops you from wasting time wondering what piece of content to produce every time something is due to be posted. By doing the strategic work of aligning your content with your business goals a couple of times per year, you will never wonder what to create again! You can also work in advance. If you're on a roll, you can produce several pieces at one time, because you know which topics are coming up next.

Some wellpreneurs feel resistance around planning their content this way. You might feel like it restricts your creative freedom or prevents you from writing about timely topics. Not so! Ultimately it's your business and you can create what you want. Having an editorial calendar just ensures that the majority of your content is totally on-target to grow your business. Occasionally when there's a topic you are really excited to write about, you can just slot that in, and push out the planned content to the next week.

Let's create your editorial calendar now.

How often did you decide to create your content? If you've decided to blog once a week on a Tuesday, then you'll want to make an editorial calendar of the next six months with one blog post idea or title listed for each Tuesday.

You can create your editorial calendar in a document or spreadsheet, or in an online or physical calendar. Do what you will USE regularly. Your editorial calendar is meant to be used every single week, so it should be easy to access and not buried in an obscure document that will get lost on your hard drive. Make it easy for yourself.

Personally I've tried numerous methods for my editorial calendar, and now I just keep it on my team's Google calendar. All the brainstorming about topics goes into Evernote, and then the final list of topics are scheduled as appointments in my calendar. That makes it really easy to see at a glance what content needs to be created. It also ensures we never have a week without a post (or in my case, without a podcast episode).

Once you have your list of ideas, the simplest approach is to take your top 10 content ideas and assign dates for when they'll be published.

If you're a bit more advanced in your marketing, you'll want to take a few other considerations into account:

- Do you have any product or program launches coming up? Is there content that fits particularly well with those topics? If so, you might want to schedule this content during the launch period.

- Are there any holiday or event tie-ins with your content?

- What are the top questions or topics your ideal customer will search for? You'll want to prioritize releasing these posts first.

Creating Your Content

Now that you have your content planned, it's time to actually create it. Here are some proven strategies to make content creation easy and effective.

Content Creation Tip 1: Schedule It

The most stressful, least productive way to create content is to wait until the day it's supposed to be published and then scramble to create and release it that same day. All bloggers have been there, and it does not set you up to do your best work.

Amanda Cook

To avoid hitting this bump, schedule content creation into your week.

Schedule an hour or two each week just to create content for your business. It doesn't matter what day it is, but block out that time, and hold it sacred, like you would any important meeting.

During your content creation time, look at your editorial calendar, pick out the next topic, and get down to creating it. Then, if you have more time left in your work block, you can either go to the next item, or create something that's fun and appealing to you at that moment. Pretty soon you'll have enough content created that you have a little backlog of content, and won't need to worry about having something to publish every week.

Content Creation Tip 2: Batching

Sometimes you get in a flow with writing, or filming videos, or recording podcasts, where you can just keep working without getting tired. Some days it's effortless and easy... other days it feels like a huge effort.

Maximize your flow states, whenever you get into them. When you have these sessions, you want to keep going and create as much content as possible!

This is easy when you have an editorial calendar — you can just keep creating items off your list!

But here is the secret: even though you've just created a lot of content, don't release it all right away. Just put it aside to "drip out" over time, according to your content schedule.

My favorite strategy to batch my content is to do it in phases. So if I'm on a roll with writing, I'll just write. I don't think about loading it into WordPress, or finding the image to go along with the post, I just keep writing. It's much easier in the future to load written blogs into my website, than it is to write them from scratch. (This is also a task that can be easily outsourced to an assistant.) So when I'm in the mood to write, I write!

I've also learned to batch my photography. I love taking photos, but when I want to shoot photos for my natural beauty blog, it seems to take the whole afternoon. First I need to make the product, then set up the lighting, then stage the photo, and finally try to take a good shot. So when I'm going to take photos, I take LOTS of photos at once (enough for several months of blog posts at once). I still get to spend the entire afternoon taking photos, but it's much more productive than setting up and shooting for one blog post at a time.

You might also consider batching other recurring content tasks. You could batch finding photos for your posts, or creating social media images, or writing social media updates, or loading posts into your website. Once you get your mind into a certain gear, it's so much quicker and easier to continue doing the same thing for several pieces of content at one time.

Content Creation Tip 3: Make Writing Easier

If you want to create written content, but you feel like it takes ages to produce each post, here is a stress-free blog writing formula to try:

1) Pick the topic that most appeals to you from your top 10 list of blog topics (or your editorial calendar).

2) Open up the program or app where you write and create a blank post or page.

3) Write a draft title — what is your article about? Don't get stuck here, we'll come back and fix it up later.

4) In the main body, write the three main points that you want to cover in the blog post. (This is flexible — if your article is about 'top five tips', then write out your five tips roughly, just so you know what you want to cover.) Put each of these main points in bold, so they become a sub-heading.

5) Write the introduction — just one paragraph which explains to the reader why this is important or relevant to them. You might want to ask a question, or relate a personal story.

6) Then get right into the heart of the blog post, and start expanding on the main points. The main points are those bold subheadings, and you just write one paragraph expanding on that point below the subheading. That's it. It's not a huge comprehensive essay, so it's OK to keep it short.

7) Revise your blog post title. Check out my copywriting resources in the Book Bonuses for more guidance.

8) Give it all a proofread for grammar, spelling and flow — and you're done!

ACTION STEPS:

- Decide what type of content you'll create, and how often.

- Use my Content Creation exercise to determine your content topics, and then organize them into an editorial calendar for the next 6 months.

- Schedule regular content creation time into your calendar.

- Create your first piece of content! Share it with us using the hashtag #wellpreneurbook

Wellpreneur Interview: Bree Argetsinger

Bree Argetsinger is the creator of The Betty Rocker. In this interview, Bree shares how she started her blog as a content platform to launch a business. Learn more at TheBettyRocker.com.

I started my blog almost five years ago because I was recovering from treating my body really horribly for a long time. I was 34, and I'd just learned how to be a healthy, balanced human. I believe that intuitively, we each know what's right for us, when we actually allow ourselves to listen. I had bypassed those signals for many years and was not doing what was right for me. So once I turned that corner, I really wanted to share — because if it was useful for me, I thought it might be useful for others as well.

My original idea was to have a Betty Rocker show. But I started with the blog to develop a platform. I also wanted to write a book. In the beginning, I wrote multiple book proposals and got lots and lots of rejections. But the entire time I continued blogging. The turning point was about one year in when I got a call from Whole Foods.

I used to shop at Whole Foods a lot, and I thought their employees were so cool. I'd talk with them while I was shopping, and one of the women used the advice from my blog to lose 50 pounds. So they called me, and I started teaching cooking classes at Whole Foods. Those classes gave me the confidence I needed to take my business seriously.

I think what set me apart in those early days was the things that I would write. I was in a lot of pain emotionally and personally trying to overcome my demons, I was healing myself with food, and I was learning to love myself and love my body. It was really inspiring for people, and so I gained a following quickly. By the time my first eBook came out, I had 10,000 followers.

I started mentioning the book in my Instagram posts a few times a week. And I started selling 100 copies a month without even trying. The book was $47, so those sales more than doubled the income that I had back then.

At the time, I was working as a structural integrationist. I had a thriving business in the motorcycle racing community. I would travel to race tracks during events and take care of the racers. I'd walk on their backs, I'd be doing adjustments, structural alignment, all kinds of great stuff, sports medicine. It was physically demanding. I was in the time for money business, so selling my first book online completely changed the game for me.

Listen to the complete interview in the Book Bonuses: WellpreneurBook.com/bonus

Chapter 9

Promotion

"Life shrinks or expands in proportion to one's courage."

— Anaïs Nin

How does the thought of promoting your business make you feel?

Excited to share, or full of dread?

Promoting your business is what people often think of as "marketing". But as you now know, this is just one little piece of the complete system. Once you've got something great to share, promotion is just about consistently getting it in front of the right people.

This step can stir up a lot of mixed feelings.

Wellpreneurs who aren't successful online are usually either promoting their business without a system behind it (which is a lot of extra effort, and when done to the extreme can turn off potential customers), or more likely, are barely promoting their businesses at all. (Sharing one link to your weekly blog post on Facebook and moving on is not an effective promotion strategy!)

If you resist promoting your business — stick with me during this chapter. You'll see that promotion doesn't have to be overly pushy or "showing off", or even look like what you've seen other people do. In this chapter you'll find a promotion strategy that puts you in front of your ideal clients everyday AND feels good for you.

Mindset Shift: Promotion Is Like Planting Seeds

Many business owners have the misconception that promotion is shouting about your business to get people to take action right now. "Buy my book!" "Check out my big sale!" "Don't miss this offer!"

That kind of promotion gets old really quickly.

If you want to build a sustainable business, then you need to develop relationships with your customers, so they *want* to hear from you! Customers who know, like and trust you are more likely to open your emails, read your offers, share your content, refer you to friends and of course, buy from you. That's what we're working towards with the Organic Growth System in this book.

Instead of only having one volume of promotion (loud — "Buy, buy, buy!"), we're going to take a different approach: Planting seeds.

Every time you promote your business, you're planting a seed that leads back to your business.

Some of these seeds stay small, others sprout slowly, and others flourish into huge, gorgeous plants.

You can't control how much they grow, but you *can* control how many seeds you plant.

That's your job with promotion, to just keep planting seeds.

What are these seeds you're going to plant? The links to your content or opt-in gift landing page.

Whether the online seed grows into a huge plant depends on how many people click through your link. You can be guided by what's working for other people, but ultimately you'll need to experiment and see where it's most effective to plant seeds so *your ideal customer* can find them.

You can plant seeds for your business every single day. You might:

- Share your new blog, video or podcast.

- Share an old blog, video or podcast that's still relevant.

- Share the landing page where people can sign up for your free gift.

- Share relevant content from other sources (which adds value to your audience because you're curating quality information for them)

- Leave a comment on a blog which links back to your website.

- Engage in a relevant group or forum, with your website mentioned in your profile.

- Write blog posts for bigger websites, with your website linked in your bio.

- Maybe you're mentioned in mainstream media, or get interviewed on a podcast, or give a workshop, or hand out business cards, or run some advertising, or have a booth at a conference, or host a webinar…

As you can see, there are plenty of things that can be used as your seeds!

Promotion is where you can really let your creativity shine. There are almost unlimited ways to promote your business. It all comes down to where your ideal customer already is, and what feels good to you.

The Secret to Effective Promotion

There's a secret to effective promotion that seems so obvious — but is often overlooked:

Where is your ideal customer ALREADY hanging out online?

It's very simple! You just need to go where your ideal customer already is.

Don't choose a promotion strategy based on what's trendy, where other wellpreneurs promote or where you think your ideal customer *should* hang out. Really consider your specific ideal customer. Where is she already hanging out on a regular basis? Where would it be easy to find large groups of your ideal customer?

Almost daily on Facebook I see wellpreneurs spending way too much time in groups specifically for other wellpreneurs! Stop trying to promote your free opt-in about health coaching to other wellpreneurs who are already health coaches — they're not your customers.

The internet is a big place. Ask your ideal customers where they hang out online (who do they follow? What are their favorite sites?). It's so much better to be the go-to expert in a smaller group, than to be one of fifty wellpreneurs trying to engage and compete for customers in a big group.

This clear identification of your ideal client helps you cut through the promotional noise.

There's no promotional platform that is better than all the others — it completely depends on your ideal customer.

Should you promote on LinkedIn? Yes, if you're targeting corporate employees and professionals, but probably not if you're targeting college students or stay-at-home moms.

Should you be on Pinterest? If you're targeting women, that could work well... but for men it's much less popular.

What about Twitter? Or Instagram? Or the new platform everyone seems to be testing? Well... is your ideal client already there? Or do you just think it's cool and *wish* she would start using it?

Let's be clear: there's nothing wrong with trying out the latest social platform. But put it in context for your business. You'll have your core promotional platforms, and those are your priority for your business.

If you have extra time, you can try out the latest platform. Maybe it'll be a hit for your audience, or maybe it won't, but as long as you're consistently promoting on your core platforms, you'll be feeding your Organic Growth System to deliver a steady stream of leads to your business.

So What, Exactly, Am I Promoting?

Every time you're posting, sharing, writing or talking about your topic, you're effectively promoting your business.

Sometimes those promotions will be direct, such as when you share your Opt-In Gift, your upcoming workshop or program, or your latest blog post.

Other times those promotions are indirect, such as when you share relevant content from other sources, or engage in a group or forum providing advice or guidance. You can also plant seeds by being an expert interview on podcasts or in the media. While you're not directly promoting your business, you're speaking as an expert on your subject matter, which leads people to visit your website.

The best promotional strategies use a blend of direct and indirect promotion. Sometimes you directly promote your content, programs and opt-ins, and other times you're adding value and engaging. It all adds up to establishing your expert authority and keeping you and your business front of mind.

Types of Promotion

To get your creative juices flowing, here are some platforms and strategies you can consider for promotion. You'll have better results if you pick two or three of these and stick with them for six months, rather than promoting a little bit everywhere. Choose based on your strengths, what feels achievable and fun, and of course, based on where your ideal client already is.

- Social Media
- Guest Posting
- Magazines or Newspapers
- Advertising
- Webinars
- Partnerships or referrals
- Talks or Workshops
- Podcast Interviews

Promotional strategies for your wellness business could fill an entire book! I'll give you a few of my favorites, based on what I've seen working for other wellpreneurs, at the time of writing, but the online world changes so quickly that you'll want to do some research on what's working on your chosen promotion platforms now. The key is that you now understand how promotion fits into your overall system — so that no matter what new platforms and promotional opportunities arise in the future, you can be smart about making sure they bring you new leads!

Now, just because your business is online doesn't mean that you should only ever do promotion online. Many wellpreneurs meet new clients in person, and then work with them online. So if you're excited about doing workshops, conferences or events, feel free to include those in your promotional plan as well.

Social Media

Social media is an easy (and often free) way to promote your business. The nuance with social media is that on most sites, you won't be successful if you just jump on and 'link bomb' the platform everyday — you have to *engage*.

Regardless of platform, it's important to understand that effective social media has two parts: Posting and Engagement.

Posting is easy to automate. You can decide when and how often you'll promote, and then set up those posts a week or two in advance. I'll share my current social media automation tool recommendations in the Book Bonuses.

Engagement can't be automated. Some people try but it looks fake and spammy — think of those generic "great pic!" comments you get on Instagram. That's fake engagement. Engagement is replying to comments, asking questions, providing helpful tips, sharing experiences and really interacting with members of your community. Try to block in 15-30 minutes per day to engage on your key platforms. Set a timer if you're worried about getting distracted, and stick to groups, platforms, hashtags etc., where your ideal customers hang out.

The big question is how to choose which social media platforms to use. You can't be everywhere, and **it's much better to have a good following and presence on one or two platforms, than to be on every platform and have no engagement or following at all.**

Here are some questions to ask yourself when choosing a social media platform:

- Does my ideal customer love this platform and use it regularly?

- Does it play to my strengths? (For example, an image-heavy platform like Instagram might not be the right fit if you hate photography or don't have an eye for design)

- Do I enjoy it?

- Am I willing to post and engage on this platform several times per week for at least a year?

For social media specifically, start by asking people in your target market which platforms they prefer. Your limited time will be best spent on a platform where lots of your ideal customers already hang out — so focus on those!

Guest Posting

Guest posting simply means that you are writing a blog post as a guest for a more popular website. This is a really effective strategy if you focus on writing for blogs or sites which are bigger than yours and that your ideal customer reads regularly. It can be a shortcut to building a targeted audience, because you get to go where your ideal customer is already!

Amanda Cook

A common mistake here is that all wellpreneurs seem to want to post on the exact same websites. Forget about where everyone else is guest posting, and again, ask your ideal customer: what blogs and websites does she read regularly? Then approach those websites about writing relevant, valuable guest posts. There's no wellpreneur gold star for having a guest post on each of the popular sites, so just do what makes sense for your business!

Magazines and Newspapers

You can also pitch to write articles or be quoted by journalists in traditional media like magazines and newspapers. This isn't as impossible as you would imagine, if you can craft a good story around your business. See the Book Bonuses for more resources here.

Webinars, Talks and Workshops

These three are very similar — in fact, a webinar is like doing a virtual talk or workshop. Don't let yourself get stuck in the mindset that "I want an online business, so I have to do everything online!" — not true. I often have met people at networking events, and then work with them through online coaching or in one of my online group programs. Don't impose imaginary rules on yourself that hold you back from finding your first clients! If you have the opportunity to speak to a group or meet people in person — do it — and send them back to your content or free opt-in gift, just like you would with anyone online!

Get Interviewed on a Podcast

As a podcast host, I can assure you that we are always looking for new guests and interesting content for our audience! Put yourself on a 'podcast tour' and pitch yourself to be a guest on podcasts.

Use the same filters as with social media and guest posting to decide where to pitch yourself. You'll want to find the podcasts that your ideal client already listens to, and those aren't necessarily the big name podcasts. Getting interviewed on big podcasts can be great to splash a logo on your website, but for lead generation, go where your potential clients already are.

Advertising

You can always pay to promote your content and your opt-in. We're seeing this on social media more frequently now — that to get your content in front of the most people, you need to pay. Advertising is too big a subject to cover here, but be aware that if you do choose to advertise, you need to be really conscious of the ROI (Return On Investment) that you're getting for your spend. Don't just throw money at advertising and assume it's working. Track, measure and adjust to make sure you're getting new audience and customers for your investment. See the Book Bonuses for my favorite advertising resources.

Promotion Power Tips

Create less, and promote more! In the content chapter, we talked about the idea of creating less content, and promoting it more. Once you have an opt-in gift and a few blog posts (or podcasts, or videos) on your site, it's time to shift your focus to promotion. Block promotion time into your calendar every week — maybe even every day! You can't be everywhere, especially when you're starting out, so it's important to choose two or three promotional platforms and really own them. Just like your target market, choose two to three places to promote, and stick with it for at least six months, engaging and promoting there several times per week. Once you've decided what kind of promotion you'd like to do, this is also where a Virtual Assistant or automation tools can help you promote consistently.

Promote your old content. Wellpreneurs are always focused on their latest content, but as your audience grows, your new subscribers won't have seen your old content — content that is still relevant and useful! So don't forget your old content in your promotion strategy. Schedule in re-promotion of old content on social media (there are tools that can help you with this — see the Book Bonuses), and also link and refer to old content from your new content (for example, linking to old podcast episodes or blog posts). You can also share older content in your email newsletters and email autoresponders. As your content backlog grows, don't discount how valuable some of your 'evergreen' posts are for new visitors. Your visitors want your best information, and if that's something you published a year ago, you shouldn't feel bad about referring them to it — it's new to them and still extremely valuable!

Automation and Systems. Promotion is a recurring task in your business. Once you find the promotion that works for your business, start to look at it as a process. What are the steps? What do you do every single day, week or month to promote your business?

For example, what are your steps to promote a new blog post? Maybe you always write three tweets with a link, and share twice on your Facebook Page using a relevant image, and then share it on a Tuesday in a specific group where your ideal client hangs out.

By creating a process around your promotion, you'll save time and make it easier to outsource in the future.

Exercise: Set Your Promotion Plan

Promotion is an area where you'll grow, evolve and change throughout your business. Keep it simple to start. You don't need to start with a "perfect" promotional plan. Do what feels achievable now, then re-evaluate in a few months. It's most important to be consistent, so do what fits your business now.

Ask yourself these questions to set your promotional plan:

1. What are you going to promote? (For example, your weekly blog post, and your opt-in gift.)

2. Which two or three platforms or types of promotion will you focus on for the next six months? (Remember to choose platforms where your ideal customers already are!)

3. Now, for each of your promotional platforms, you'll want to decide:

- How often will you post content or links?
- How often will you engage with your audience there?
- What would success look like for you on this platform? How will you measure success?
- What support, tools, automation or help do you need to regularly promote your business on this platform?

Write down your promotional plan and keep it simple. It's all an experiment, especially at the beginning as you find the platforms and the messages that resonate with your audience. Have fun with it!

ACTION STEPS:

- Answer the questions in the "Getting Started with Promotion" section.

- Schedule your first promotion in your calendar!

Wellpreneur Interview: Meghan Telpner

Meghan Telpner is a Toronto-based author, speaker, nutritionist, and founder of the Academy of Culinary Nutrition. In this interview she shares her own experience with creating content and how she learned that going viral on social media isn't always the answer. Learn more at MeghanTelpner.com.

I've always had a business of some sort. I started when I was 11 years old selling scrunchies that I had sewn myself. In university, I started a women's travel magazine called Chicks Abroad. That parlayed into travels, which resulted in an illness that got me to nutrition school, and that was what propelled me into the business I have now. I loved nutrition school. I learned a ton but still didn't know how to cook, and I really wanted to build a community around the idea of good food, good conversation and community.

That's what ignited the idea for the cooking school that I had here in Toronto in our loft. Then we grew beyond the boundaries of what this 600-square-foot, brick and mortar space could accommodate. We had more people wanting to join than we could fit (and that I had the energy to teach) every single night. So we started transitioning to the online model that we have now. I'll still do the occasional in-person class here in the kitchen just because I love it. It's so fun and I love getting to meet people face-to-face.

But the majority of our teaching is now video-based online.

When I started to transition the business online, I had no idea what I was doing. I think if I'd known where this was going to go, I'd have thought, "Man, that's way too much work!" I think there's a misconception that having an online business is easy. People think that it's easy to scale, with lots of passive revenue - but that's a *huge* misconception.

Did I have any idea we were going to have a global school with students in over 40 countries? Not a chance. That was so far from what I thought was possible. By moving one step at a time, self-funding, and growing the business as we had the infrastructure and resources (both technically online and with my team to do it), has allowed it to evolve to a level that I never thought possible.

Everyone always asks me: "Where do you think it's going to go?" I have no idea because I think that what we imagine, or where we imagine ourselves to be five years from now, is self-limiting. It's so much smaller than what we're actually capable of when we're going through the processes of producing, creating, and putting it out there every single day.

I think a big challenge that entrepreneurs have is that they set high expectations for themselves in such a short, aggressive span of time, that it's impossible for them to achieve. Often they get discouraged and quit too soon. You can only do what you can do in a day. I learned this lesson, ironically, on a farm, because how do you end your day on the farm? There is always work to do. The farmer told me: "Tomorrow, there will be more work to do and you continue. You just do what you can do until your day is done, and you balance it out with how you want to live your life."

For entrepreneurs starting today, the biggest challenge is that there's so much out there already. What will help you break through that noise is honing in on what makes you uniquely awesome, your unique interests and views, being brave enough to voice an opinion that may not be the popular one (but it's yours), and putting out really high quality work. It's not just about making sure you get your two posts a week, with 500 words, a recipe, an SLR photograph, SEO tags and all of that; none of that matters.

When you actually provide deep content that is relevant to your community, *that* is what will build an audience for you. Spamming your reader's feeds with seven new posts a week isn't going to do it. That is going to get you unsubscribed and unfollowed because you can't possibly put out quality content that quickly.

As an example, we recently had an older blog post go viral. We had something like 19,000 shares on Facebook, but no spike in subscribers. To me, that says a lot. It's never been my goal to win the social media popularity contest. You can throw thousands of dollars at Facebook ads and get tons of likes on your page, but not get any real results in your business. My feeling is that with quality content, it may not get shared a thousand times, but if it brings 100 people to your site who opt-in and become loyal community members, those 100 people are worth a thousand times more than 19,000 shares on Facebook. Those are people who really want to engage with you and what you're offering. Part of it is just ignoring the numbers that people can see and focusing on quality content, as opposed to the quantity.

Listen to the complete interview in the Book Bonuses:
WellpreneurBook.com/bonus

Wellpreneur Expert Interview: Janet Murray

Janet Murray is a journalist, editor and PR expert. In this interview, she shares advice for pitching your idea to the media. Learn more about Janet at JanetMurray.co.uk.

The first step in getting media coverage is to ask yourself what you're *actually* trying to achieve, rather than just saying that you want to be in magazines or newspapers.

Most business owners I work with in health and wellness are looking to get a book deal or attract clients. So decide on your objective, and then ask yourself where you'll find those people. What are they watching, reading or listening to?

You might dream about being featured in *Marie Claire Magazine* or *The New York Times*, but if that's not where your audience is, it could be a waste of your resources. It's really about focusing on the publications where your audience already is.

So, once you've decided on the publications, you need to get three or four months of copies of the publication and really study the content. Look at what kind of stories they cover, what topics they're interested in. What ideas do you have that could fit into the type of topics they already cover? There's quite a lot of thinking and planning before you even start pitching your story idea.

The key to a successful pitch is to put aside what *you're* interested in, and give journalists what *they* want. That's why it's so important to notice what types of stories they're running already, and what topics they regularly cover.

A common mistake is finding an idea that *you* think is interesting, and just assuming the media will care about it. Business owners often want to talk about their new product, but journalists are not there to publicize your business.

Instead of thinking about yourself and what you will get out of the coverage, start by thinking how you can help the journalists.

With this approach you're not pitching them, you're not begging them for coverage — you're talking to them and you're trying to understand them. It's about sincerity, and stories that really come from the heart, that people can really connect with.

Ask yourself what people would be interested in around your business. This often requires thinking creatively. I recently saw a great example of this in *The Huffington Post*. The article was about the fact that a running magazine had a plus-sized model on the front of it. It was a really interesting opinion piece, and at the bottom of the article I saw that the author actually ran a fitness company.

This is a great example of selling your company through PR. She's obviously bringing attention to herself and what she does, but her article isn't directly about her business. The article is about what she stands for. When you approach journalists from that point of view, you'll often be successful.

As another example, I had a story in *The Guardian's* "Women in Leadership" section recently which really seemed to resonate with people. It was about how a few years ago I had an office and staff, building up a PR consultancy, but it just felt like too much. So I decided to return to being a solopreneur. The article was about that journey and about how I feel like more of a leader now since that transition.

Because the article was more about my mission and values, I've had such great engagement with it. I think that's the sweet spot when you're looking for coverage. It's not just about thinking your business is wonderful. Everybody thinks their business is wonderful. It's more about what you stand for and what stories you can share around that. That's how your pitches will be successful with journalists.

Listen to the complete interview in the Book Bonuses: WellpreneurBook.com/bonus

Wellpreneur Interview: Adina Grigore

Adina Grigore is founder and CEO of natural skincare brand S. W. Basics and author of Skin Cleanse. In this interview, she shares how her skincare business got its first big break through publicity. Learn more about Adina at SWBasicsOfBK.com.

After studying nutrition I was working as a personal trainer and holistic health counselor, and loved what I was doing. I fell into running a skincare brand for two reasons.

The first was very personal to me. I have very, very sensitive skin. I can't use most of what's on the market, and when I started getting healthier and living more holistically, I wanted to do the same for my skin.

It forced me to get in the kitchen to solve the problem on my own. Once I had made some products that really worked for me, I realized there was a huge gaping void in the market. The food world was really focused on wellness, but it wasn't the case in skincare. I wanted the products I was making for myself to be available to everyone. I just felt like it was the right opportunity. I did a lot of research on what else was available, and then I went for it.

I started out really slow. I was working full-time. I think I was really lucky that I had chosen to do nutrition because I used nutrition as my main event for a very, very long time. At the time I was doing workshops for nutrition, so I just transitioned those into DIY skincare workshops.

Amanda Cook

Workshops are a great way of gauging response, but it was scary to do them at the time. Even though I was just teaching people how to make skincare, I wasn't even selling anything! But it was largely those workshops that made me decide to sell the products, because people would line up at the end of the workshops asking to buy them.

From there, I took another small step forward and launched an Etsy shop. I also did local farmer's markets and flea markets. And actually, I did horribly on Etsy. If I had decided based on Etsy whether I should move forward, I probably would've quit.

The thing that's nice about products is (as far as self-promoting), it's a little bit easier because you just send people free samples. At the beginning, that's just what it was. Get it in the hands of everyone and anyone, and see what they think and how it goes.

One of these things included sending it to press people. One big break for us was sending it to Gwyneth Paltrow's team, and she featured us. They put us on their website and we had no business being on there — I mean, we were still handwriting our labels, but it was huge. It was a huge deal, and it was huge sales-wise. It's huge to this day, actually. This was in 2011. People still come to us having found us on there.

The second big thing that happened for us was our first store, and it was from my boss at the time who owned Pure Food and Wine, and One Lucky Duck. I was working there and she took a really big leap of faith on us and featured us in the store.

When you get your first store and your first press piece, it's the thing that sort of gets you started. From there, other people find you and other stores find you, and you're able to say, "Look, I'm in the store.

We have this press feature." Those are the two big things that made us feel like, wow, this is really happening!

Listen to the complete interview in the Book Bonuses:
WellpreneurBook.com/bonus

Chapter 10

Nurture and Convert

"The glue that holds all relationships together, including the relation-ship between the leader and the led, is trust, and trust is based on integrity."

— Brian Tracy

Are you familiar with the Online Business Fairytale?

It goes something like this…

Your workday starts with a fresh coconut water as you check your email from your balcony overlooking a tropical beach. Ooh, you made $2,000 overnight! Brilliant. You do a quick check-in with your virtual assistant in the Philippines to make sure this week's blog posts are on-track. Then, you have a coaching call with a client in the USA, which you do via video chat, still on your balcony. After your client call, you're off to yoga class, then have a green smoothie, and then come home to see that your virtual team has prepared everything for your big detox program launch next week, so all you need to do is deliver the webinar. Life is good!

If my Facebook newsfeed is anything to go by, it feels like an online business *should* be that way.

If you're in a lot of entrepreneur (and 'wantrapreneur') groups on Facebook, you'll see updates almost daily that say: "OMG guys! I sent one email and made six figures overnight!"

When you read that update, no matter how pleased you were with your own business just 30 seconds ago, you now spiral into doubt and shame. What's wrong with me? Is that for real? What does she know that I don't? Why am I so bad at this? Maybe I should just give up!

All I can say is — ick. Many of these posts are thinly-veiled attempts to find business coaching clients rather than genuine celebration of achievement: "Yay for me! If you want to make this much money too, I can teach you my secrets, just send me a message / come to my webinar / join my list."

Let's clear the air around what's possible (and what's hype) for your online wellness business. Then we'll learn how you can turn your growing list of email subscribers into a happy community of paying clients.

But first: is that beach-living, yoga-going, virtual-clients-and-team scenario I described above possible for wellpreneurs? Definitely. But will *every day* in your business look like that? Definitely not!

Second, let's do a reality check on those braggy posts about sending one email and instantly making some major amount of revenue. The truth is, it's never just a single email.

Using the Organic Growth System, you will be able to send an email, and immediately see revenue come into your business.

BUT what you're not seeing in these status updates is the work that happened BEFORE that email was sent. The work that builds up the audience of people who know, like and trust you. That sales email is just the final step in the flow from website visitor to paying client.

The unknown factor in these updates is HOW the person posting got to that number. The amount of revenue you generate is tied to the price of your products, and the size of your audience. When someone says she sent one email to make $10,000 — did she sell one consulting package at $10,000? 1,000 copies of her $10 eBook? 103 copies of her $97 eCourse?

Let's take the $97 eCourse as an example. If 2% of the people she emailed about the offer actually purchased, she would need to email 5,000 active subscribers to sell 103 copies of her course. Is this achievable? Absolutely, yes. But does it happen immediately with "just sending one email"? No way. It's never just about the one email. It's about the system that's been put in place, and consistently fueling that system on a daily, weekly and monthly basis. The system is the secret sauce that separates successful wellpreneurs from those who struggle online. And if you've come with me this far in the book, this chapter is the final piece to that system!

From Nurturing to Selling

Think about a recent shopping experience. There are different types of shopping trips, right? Sometimes you're just shopping for fun, wandering around stores and "just looking." You might take this kind of shopping trip for a lot of reasons. You could be bored, you could have time to kill before an appointment, you might want inspiration and ideas, you might be doing some research for a future purchase — but whatever the reason, on this kind of shopping trip you're not really motivated to buy. You're just looking.

On other shopping trips you've got a goal in mind. Maybe that summer wedding is just a few weeks away and you need an outfit, or all your socks have holes, or your air conditioner broke during a heat wave, or you need something to cook for dinner tonight. In times like these, you're shopping with the intention of buying — and on these kind of trips there's a much higher probability that you'll leave the store having made a purchase.

If, during your "just looking" trip, a salesperson keeps reappearing and urging you to "buy this" or "how about this one?" — it gets really annoying. You only want to look, not buy! If that salesperson is really pushy, you might just leave the store, or even decide not to shop there in the future. But, if you're on a buying trip, having a salesperson do the same thing can be REALLY helpful.

If they offer to help, then you tell them you're looking for a new white T-shirt, and the salesperson goes off to pick up their three best-selling white T-shirts and brings them to you, it's perfect! It's easy and saves time.

We can apply the same approach to our email subscribers and our offers. People visit your website, read your content, and join your email list for a ton of different reasons — usually NOT because they want to buy health coaching services right now.

Something about your content and your opt-in gift caught their attention. It hit on their needs and aspirations, so they joined your email list, but they're not necessarily ready to buy at this exact moment. This is where nurturing starts. Your job, Wellpreneur, is to keep in touch with them, keep offering value and connection, and to make offers on your products and services. Then when they're ready to buy, they'll think of you first!

The Nurture and Convert phase of your Organic Growth System happens continually. As long as someone is subscribed to your list, you'll be building your relationship with them, and making offers. You're nurturing that relationship, and will eventually convert them into a paid customer. It's a never-ending cycle. Even when a subscriber becomes a paying customer, the cycle doesn't end. You're still building your relationship further, and making *additional* offers. In fact, existing customers are usually the best future customers, because they've already experienced the benefits of your work!

So think of your nurture and conversion process as a long term, ongoing strategy.

Mindset Shift: Your Subscribers are People, Not Numbers

It's easy to get caught up in the numbers of email marketing. List size, open rates, click rates… The reality is that a real person is behind each email address. A person who discovered your business, liked what you had to say, and trusted you enough to give you access to their email inbox. Don't break that trust.

You're not going to be one of those spammy, scammy marketers selling anything and everything, or who only emails your list when you have something to sell. You're going to be different, ethical, engaged and appreciative of your community. After all — *these are your people!*

That doesn't mean you can't sell anything — just the opposite. You have a business and will absolutely sell things. But you'll also provide value. You'll give them quality information, and a connection to people like them, and occasionally offer valuable products, which makes it worthwhile (and hopefully fun!) to be a part of your email community.

It Starts with the Buying Cycle

In my previous corporate life, we talked a lot about the buying cycle. My boss always wanted to know: what *stage* was the buyer in? Were they prepared to write a purchase order, did they have an allocated budget, or were they still comparing us to our competitors? We had these stages mapped out in exquisite detail.

In our wellpreneur businesses, we don't need to be as strict about defining buying phases — but you'll still want to apply the buying cycle to your business. As you have more sales conversations with potential customers, you'll start to see buying stages appear naturally.

The basic stages of a buying cycle are:

- Awareness: buyer is aware that she has a problem, and that you can provide valuable information or solutions around it.

- Consideration: buyer is motivated to fix the problem, and is actively looking for solutions — from you and your competitors.

- Preference: buyer makes a decision that she wants to buy the solution, and that she'll buy it from you.

- Purchase: she buys your solution!

- Repurchase: she uses and reviews your solution, and is open to buying additional products and services.

As you get more experienced with email nurturing, you can get quite sophisticated in determining which phase a customer is in (based on her behavior) and offering her specific emails at these times.

But let's not get stuck on that for now. **The key takeaway now is to understand that not everyone is ready to buy immediately when they join your list — and that you want to offer them content which 'nurtures' them along this buying cycle, builds your relationship with them AND make offers.**

Two Approaches to Email Nurturing

Here's the big idea behind email nurturing: Since not everyone is ready to buy immediately when they join your list, you need a strategy to build your relationship, offer value, and make occasional offers until they are ready.

There are two approaches to email nurturing: newsletters and autoresponders. You've probably heard that you must have an email newsletter, but I find it's often easier to start with an autoresponder. Let's look at the difference between these two approaches.

Email newsletters are sent out to your entire email list at the same time (sometimes also called a 'broadcast' email or the dreadful 'email blast'.) An email newsletter often includes a little note from you, your latest blog posts or content, upcoming events, and an offer for your products and services. The key point is that you'll be writing your email newsletter once per week or month (whatever frequency you're going to send it out), and when you send it, that's it. Email newsletters are one-time-only. If someone joins your list the next day, they'll have to wait until the next week or month to get your next email newsletter.

Autoresponders are an automated sequence of emails that start whenever someone subscribes to your email list. This means that every new subscriber gets the same introductory experience to your business. It doesn't matter when they join — Tuesday or Friday, at 3PM or 3AM — when they join your list, they'll get a welcome email, and then they'll get a specific series of emails dripped out to them over the coming days and weeks.

There are three huge benefits of autoresponders:

1) **Intentional customer experience.** You'll know that new subscribers are seeing your very best content first, and you're providing maximum value, because everyone is getting the same email sequence when they join.

2) **Increased engagement.** People love autoresponders (when they're done ethically) because they receive an immediate piece of content when they join, followed by regular, valuable content that helps them — it's a strange experience to sign up for an email list and then not hear anything for a month! A new subscriber is motivated and wants to learn about the topic, so an autoresponder lets you deliver on that immediately, regardless of when they sign up.

3) **It's easier for you.** You set up the autoresponder sequence once, and people get it whenever they subscribe! You can send email newsletters less frequently (focusing around timely information like events), because you know new subscribers are hearing from you automatically.

You usually have to pay for an email marketing service to use autoresponders (as opposed to email newsletters which are sometimes free, depending on the service). But for a small list this cost is usually very affordable, and just think of the time you'll save *not* creating email newsletters each week — it pays for itself!

You also need to review your autoresponder periodically to see how it's performing, and to update it with your latest and greatest valuable content.

And if you do decide to send a broadcast email or newsletter, remember that new subscribers are automatically receiving your autoresponder content. Exclude them from these broadcasts, or at least keep it to a minimum, so you don't overwhelm them with email!

Create Your First Autoresponder

As we're in the process of building out your Organic Growth System path from website visitor to paying client, it's the ideal opportunity to create your first autoresponder. Let's start by creating an autoresponder for your Opt-In Gift.

The idea with this "Welcome Sequence" autoresponder is that every new customer will get the same introduction to your business. They'll get to know you over a few emails, and you can help them get the most out of your opt-In gift.

No matter which type of digital product you've chosen from your opt-in gift, try to shift your thinking from "I just need to send them an eBook and I'm done!" to understanding that **in online marketing, everything is a sequence.**

Whether you're creating an eBook or resource list or PDF guide, don't think of it simply as delivering that guide. Every opt-in is the start of a sequence of communication with your new subscriber. If you are delivering an eBook immediately upon signup, then you also want to think about the next three email communications they'll get from you to move them further along the path towards becoming a customer.

Some types of opt-ins lend themselves naturally to being a sequence. For example, if you're offering a simple email course, you'll deliver a piece of content everyday for a certain number of days (or weeks), so it's already a sequence. But if it's an eBook, you want to think about what happens after you deliver the eBook, so they get the most out of it.

Here's an example of how a welcome sequence might look for a coach offering a free eBook.

Sample Welcome Sequence (for an eBook):

- Day 0 — Subscriber receives link to download eBook.

- Day 1 — Subscriber receives a question: Did you read the eBook? You can mention one part that is especially relevant and share a story about it from your own life.

- Day 2 — Subscriber learns how to apply what they've learned to their life, you can share a client story, and offer a free strategy session.

- Day 5 — You keep the momentum going with another tip on how they can go further using this information, and offer a free strategy session.

Finally they drop into your normal periodic email newsletter communication.

How long should your sequence be? It depends! Some online marketers have extensive email sequences that continue for six months or more, offering all of their products and services based on which links the prospects click! But I don't recommend you do this yet. At this point, you don't know enough about your potential customer or which of your products will be most appealing — so writing a lengthy email sequence would be a waste of your time. Start with three or four emails, and let them run for a few months to check their performance before writing more.

Some options you could include in your follow up sequence:

- Highlight one idea or action from your opt-in gift with how it can help them

- Tell a story about your own life using the ideas from your opt-in

- Share a case study of a customer who got results using the opt-in

- Ask them a question, and have them 'hit reply' to your email to answer it!

- Offer a low-priced entry level product

- Offer a free 'strategy session' with you (as part of your process to enroll coaching clients)

- Gently introduce them to your business and what you do (but in the context of the opt-in and how it helps them!)

Outline your follow up sequence, and then write it. Much like the process of creating your opt-in gift, write it in a plain text document so you can focus purely on the content. Once the content is finalized, you can think about setting it up in your email marketing program.

Put your sequence aside for a few hours or overnight, and then read through the entire sequence again, as if you were a new subscriber. Do the emails make sense in that sequence? Do they help you get more from the opt-in gift? Do they sound warm, friendly and show your personality? Have you included at least one 'Call To Action' where you ask the customer to reply to you, book a strategy session or buy something?

Don't stress about this. It is impossible to create a 'perfect' autoresponder sequence. The goal in this step is to create your first sequence, let it run for a couple of months, and then look at the metrics to see how it's performing before making changes. You will always adjust and improve your autoresponder over time — so just create what you can now, and add to it over time.

Don't Forget the CTA

Make sure you include a Call to Action (CTA) in every email. A Call To Action is an invitation for the reader to take the specific action you are leading them to in each email.

Many wellpreneurs make the mistake of including too many CTAs in their emails. If you ask a reader to take several actions at one time, she'll probably feel overwhelmed and do nothing. Instead, you should focus each email around a single CTA — the one most important action you want her to take right now.

Call To Action ideas…

- Click here to continue reading

- Click to Tweet

- Click to share with your friends on social media

- Hit reply and tell me...

- Click here and Like my Facebook page

- Register for my event

- Buy this product

- Book your complimentary strategy session

Whichever CTA you choose for an email, make it obvious and easy for the reader to take action.

Make it Obvious: I often see new wellpreneurs hiding their CTA, because they don't want to be pushy or salesy. But the reality is that most people are distracted and quickly skimming your emails, so you need to tell them specifically how to take the next step: "Click here", "Like this", "Share with your friends", "Hit Reply". If you don't tell them directly what to do, they won't know and they won't spend time to think about it — they'll just leave. Clearly state your CTA at least twice in your email — possibly putting the link in bold on a separate line so it really stands out.

Make it Easy: Your email subscribers are busy and even if they love your brand, they probably won't spend more than a few seconds acting on your CTA. So if your CTA is "Share This Blog Post!" don't make them click through to the website, copy the URL, go to Facebook, think of what to write in the post, paste the link, and then share it — no one will do that. Instead, imagine if you had one single link that's a pre-configured 'sharing' link which automatically opens Facebook and pre-populates the update with your blog post — one click and it's shared. Easy! There are tools and plugins which enable this one-click share functionality — use them. Make it easy for your fans to spread the word about you.

The Email Newsletter Strategy

If you do decide to do an email newsletter for your business (which means that you're broadcasting time-sensitive emails to your subscribers), then please — keep it simple.

Try to avoid creating new content for an email newsletter because once you send it, it's gone! Instead, share what you've already created. Share links to your latest content, customer success stories, upcoming events and time-limited offers. You can start your email with a short personal welcome, and then get into sharing your content.

Keep it simple, and remember the goal of the email newsletter: to keep you front of mind with your potential customers, build your relationship and make offers.

How Often Should I Email My List?

Somewhere between weekly and monthly, on a regular basis.

If you've created an autoresponder, you may want to taper off the frequency over time. Start by emailing daily in the beginning, and then slow it down to every few days, and then finally to once a week ongoing.

If you're sending an email newsletter, once or twice a month works well.

Of course, whenever you're running a time-sensitive promotion (like a product launch), you'll email daily or more for a short period. Then after the launch, just go back to your normal frequency.

It's a good idea to set expectations about email frequency up front. When someone joins your list, tell them how often they can expect to hear from you. You can do this on the signup form itself, or in your first autoresponder email to them. Something as simple as "You'll hear from me about once a week." will do the trick.

Despite your best intentions, at some point you might let your list "go cold." That means you've gone more than two months without emailing your list. When this happens, don't freak out. Accept that it happened, and reestablish contact with your list by delivering value. If you have let your list grow cold, send two or three value-packed emails to rebuild your relationship before you make an offer!

When Should I Email?

This is different for every market.

Think about your potential customer's routine. Is she at an office during the week or at home? If she has an office job, on Mondays she is probably focused on working, but as the week went on (especially in the afternoons) she'll be more likely to read a personal email (except on Friday afternoons when everyone just wants to wrap things up and go home). What about your customer? What's the difference in routine for a stay-at-home-mom or a 20-something guy? Know your customer and send at the times that they'll be most likely to read.

Once you get into a routine with your emails, you can test sending on different days and times to see which get the highest open and click rates. You'll want to pre-schedule your emails so they send at a specific time — you don't need to be online to click the "send" button right then!

Should I Send HTML or Plain Text Emails?

Most email programs give you the option to send 'pretty' HTML emails with images and formatting, or plain text. Plain text emails are more like what you receive from a friend. HTML emails are what most big brands use, and include their logo, formatting and lots of images. Successful email marketers have used both strategies, and there's no right answer on which style to use.

There are two schools of thought here. One is that if the big brands use HTML, then your small business can seem bigger and more professional by sending HTML emails too.

The other side is that consumers are trained to identify HTML emails as sales emails. So they're more likely to delete or disregard your email if it's HTML. Whereas a plain text email might look as if it's coming from a friend, so people are more willing to read it.

At the beginning, this is a personal choice. The most important factor is to stay in touch with your subscribers regularly! So do whatever feels easiest to you right now. Over time you can test HTML vs. plain text emails by sending both types and checking the metrics for which gets better engagement from your audience.

No matter what type of email you send, make sure it's mobile-friendly. Test it yourself by sending it to yourself and reading it on your phone. Is it easy to read? Can you click the links?

Email Engagement with Replies

Wouldn't it be cool to make your emails feel more like a conversation? There's an easy way to do this, but you have to train your subscribers from the very start: just ask them to reply to you.

Start this engagement by asking a question in your first or second email. Specifically tell them to "Hit reply and tell me..." Most people won't reply, but some will — and that's an amazing chance to make a personal connection with a subscriber.

Another benefit of this strategy is that when a subscriber replies, it shows their email program that you're an important contact, so your emails are more likely to appear in their inbox instead of their spam folder!

If you try this strategy, don't do it in every email because it will lose its appeal. Alternate asking questions with other Calls to Action, and make sure you're sending from an email address that can receive replies! (You can usually choose the email address that you send from in your email program — so make sure it's an inbox you can check!) Most importantly, when people reply to you, you need to respond back to them! Show them there's an actual person on the other side of that email address.

How Much to Sell in Your Emails

There are two purposes to your emails:

1. Build the know/like/trust factor

2. Convert subscribers into paying customers (sell them something!)

Most wellpreneurs fall into one of two camps — they either deliver value all the time, and never make an offer, or they sell in every single email. In both cases, these wellpreneurs are not making as many sales as they would like, because they've lost the balance.

They're both caused by different issues. The wellpreneur who delivers value but never sells usually has an underlying fear that her audience will dislike her if she is too 'salesy'. So she builds up a habit of delivering amazing free information, which makes it even worse when she does decide to sell something, because now her audience is only expecting free things — so they are a bit surprised to be asked to pay!

Mindset Shift Around Making Offers: If you give real value in your emails, but rarely make an offer, you're actually keeping your readers from fully solving their problems.

Is it possible for you to fully solve their problems through your free emails, blogs, videos etc? Shouldn't they have the chance to go further and allow you to help them with your 1:1 services, group programs, or in-depth training courses?

If you don't offer it, they won't know that you have these, and certainly won't think about buying them. You know your products and services better than anyone else, and it's up to you to offer them to your customer at the points when she might need them. It's not realistic to expect that a customer will remember all of your products and services and then suddenly think "Oh, I think right now this 21-day detox program from Amanda is exactly what I need" — it's up to you to offer your programs regularly in your email sequence.

Don't worry — you won't be selling all the time. A successful email sequence has a balance of delivering value and making offers. You can still help subscribers for free with your emails... but then you'll give them the chance to upgrade and go further with you by buying a paid product or service.

The second type of wellpreneur is the one who just sells in every single email. While there are some internet marketers who email a lot, and sell a lot, you see a different problem with wellpreneurs. Here's how it works: You're focused on building your list or working with clients or just elsewhere in your business. You're "too busy" to email your list (which is actually never true, it's a question of priorities). Then one day you realize that you're out of money, or out of clients. Panic! So you email your list with a few emails pitching your programs and services. These emails usually don't convert very well, so you scramble around trying to find clients. Once you do, then the pressure is off, although you feel a little guilty for not emailing your list more regularly, so you send an email newsletter, and then you get busy again and go quiet, until you run low on money again...

I don't have to tell you that this second strategy just does not work. You're not building a good relationship with your list, and when you do make offers, your subscribers have often forgotten about you, so they're less likely to buy.

Again, this is why autoresponder sequences are awesome. You can set up an email sequence that delivers a mix of value and offers, and then just let it run. Over time you can adjust the sequence based on metrics and feedback, and you can expand it to add new products and services.

As long as you have a welcome sequence set up which makes an initial offer to new subscribers, you have a complete path to bring more of the right people to your website and turn them into paying clients.

Nurturing and conversion is an ongoing process in your wellness business, and it's something that you'll certainly refine over time. But done in the right way, it's a great introduction to your brand, and develops new clients for your business.

ACTION STEPS:

- Decide how often you're going to contact your email list.

- Will you setup an autoresponder or an email newsletter? Both?

- What is the first offer you'll make?

- Create your first email newsletter or set up your welcome sequence autoresponder.

Amanda Cook

Wellpreneur Expert Interview:
Matthew Kimberley

Matthew Kimberley helps consultants, coaches and service providers to sell more. In this interview, he shares sales strategies that can work for wellpreneurs, even if you dislike the idea of selling! Learn more about Matthew at MatthewKimberley.com.

A salesperson initiates a sale, or makes it happen, unlike an order taker who simply waits to receive orders. Which are you in your business? The reason we're often afraid to initiate a sale, is because we don't want to change our relationship with the person in front of us.

Here's an example of how people who hate selling think: "I've just met you, and we're getting along really well. I think you'd make a great prospect for my business. But I'm going to wait until you approach me about it, because if I ask you for a sale, you'll no longer see me as a nice guy. You'll see me as someone who is going to trick you into a commercial relationship."

But I believe that is nonsense. You'd have to be really ignorant to damage a relationship by simply asking someone to become a customer. Yes, we do occasionally get pissed off with salespeople who are too pushy and don't get the message we're sending them. Especially when they say: "Can I ask you why you're not interested?" That's the worst!

But most of us won't do that. Most of us won't keep pushing because we've got high levels of emotional intelligence. So let's reframe this situation:

You're having a conversation with a prospect, and you wonder what the prospect is thinking. Are they having a pleasant conversation with me? Yes. Are they exhibiting signals that they would potentially be a good customer or a good client for me? Yes, they are. Okay, well let's not pass on that opportunity. Let's ask them if they'd like to work together or even better, just make them aware it's an option.

Then let's see how that statement lands. It's almost guaranteed that if we do it right, our prospect will not be offended, they will not be upset, they will not be pissed off. They will probably be curious. And if they exhibit interest that they'd like to find out more, then you have the opportunity to present your solutions.

We don't like to change the nature of the relationship with our prospect, because we think they're going to be angry, upset, pissed off. Even though we know that's not actually the case. When was the last time that you were pissed off when somebody asked you to buy something? When was the last time you were angry when somebody said, "Hey, you should totally check out the program that's done by this guy, because it's great." Or, "Hey, you should definitely have a chat with my personal trainer because she's fantastic." Or "Hey, my nutritionist is awesome. Do you want to meet her?" The answer is normally, "Yes, thank you for thinking of me. That would be great." Rather than, "I'm so offended that you spoke to me."

We can present ourselves in such a way where we're just going to say, "Listen, I'm a nutritionist." Oh, that's great. Tell me about being a nutritionist. "Well, what I do is I help people go from feeling generally pretty rotten to feeling awesome all day long."

"Oh, that sounds fantastic." It really is. "Listen, do you want to hear a little bit more about my program, or do you think that'll be something that'll be great for you?" "Yeah, sure." Alright, well, here we go. Let me enter into my pitch. Let me have a conversation with you about it. That's it. That's how it goes. It's super simple. It's about identifying the buying signals or the interest signals. Interest is qualification. You have to qualify your prospects. When they're exhibiting signals or signs of interest, then we have the opportunity to move in and have a conversation with them.

It's not about talking them through a sales page, or standing up in front of them with a PowerPoint presentation. Getting them to sign there and then, it's just about letting people know how they can invest in you. And if they like you, and they trust you, and they need what you've got to offer, and they have the funds or they have access to the funds, then they should be able to become your client.

Listen to the complete interview in the Book Bonuses:
WellpreneurBook.com/bonus

Wellpreneur Interview: Nisha Moodley

Nisha Moodley is a women's leadership coach. In this interview she shares the importance of patience in your business (including with sales!), and how to start creating the life you want now. Learn more about Nisha at NishaMoodley.com.

I often see entrepreneurs being impatient with the process. Running a business is a journey. I've been doing this for almost seven years now. Once I had a client who did five initial consultations and no one signed up. She wanted to quit. I told her to do 50 more consultations and get 50 more no's. After you get 50 no's, then let's talk about quitting. Over the next few months she did 50 more consultations, and of course by the end of it she had a full client roster. There's an element of stick-with-it-ness that results in success. You need to be patient with your business, it can take time!

That being said, I've also found that in the pursuit of freedom, you don't need to be patient. Many people who want freedom do the exact opposite of freedom: they wait.

They might have a dream to create a business where they travel and work from their laptop, take lots of courses, spend more time with their family and deepen their spiritual practice. But they put it off until they hit certain goals, like making a certain amount of revenue or launching their website.

I tried this way of working myself. I did hit six-figures in revenue. And you know what? I still didn't have any more time for my husband or family. Then the business grew more, and my free time still didn't happen.

Amanda Cook

It wasn't until I decided that my life is happening *right now* that things changed. Yes, you can have a beautiful future vision, but how do you want to feel right now, and how can you readjust your life in service of that? How can you infuse the things that you desire into your life right now?

If you want to spend more time with your family and friends? Start today, right now.

Listen to the complete interview in the Book Bonuses:
WellpreneurBook.com/bonus

Chapter 11

Making it Happen

"I realized early on that success was tied to not giving up. Most people in this business gave up and went on to other things. If you simply didn't give up, you would outlast the people who came in on the bus with you."

– Harrison Ford

What's your favorite form of procrastination? Maybe you...

- Get an intense urge to clean the house or organize your sock drawer?

- Decide to "work" on social media, but really get lost in the news feed?

- Suddenly become super-productive crossing 10 unimportant-but-easy tasks off your list?

- Decide to play just "one quick game" on your phone?

- Work out?

- Eat chocolate?

Since going full-time in my business, I've discovered that if there's a big gnarly task I'm avoiding, I suddenly become super efficient at doing lots of tasks that actually don't matter. In fact, I spent most of the first year of my business doing this (in addition to those few months developing the website course that didn't sell well!). I was always super busy, working all the time — but didn't have much to show for it in terms of audience or financial results.

At this point, you know everything you need to know to find your first paying clients online.

The question is: are you going to make it happen for your online wellness business? Or will online marketing be added to the bottom of a never ending to-do list?

Here's the truth:

- There is always more work to be done.

- Marketing is never "finished."

- There are 100 tasks and tweaks you could work on at any time in your online wellness business, but only a few of them will bring in more revenue and clients.

At the end of the day, it's not having the most marketing, technology or business knowledge that will determine your success — but rather, how quickly you implement what you've learned and take action.

So let's make a plan of action for your wellness business.

How Do I Know Where to Focus?

Rather than trying to set up all of your online marketing at once, print off the Organic Growth System diagram from the Book Bonuses, and working through it step by step.

Here's the order of priority to set up (or optimize) your online marketing:

1. Email list. First, do you have an email list setup? No? There's your top priority. Do that today. It's quick and easy (you can see my current recommended tools in the Book Bonuses.) Read more about this in Chapter 6.

2. Free gift or opt-in offer. If you have an email list set up, then the next question is: do you have a great free gift that's valuable and enticing to your ideal client? (If you have a free gift, but it's kind of lame and no one is signing up for it, go back to the drawing board and create something that appeals to your ideal client.) Read more about this in Chapter 7.

3. Nurturing and Conversion (newsletter or autoresponder). If you've got an email list and free gift, then look at how you're engaging with your list. What's your nurturing strategy? Do you actually send an email newsletter regularly? If so, then go a step further and create an autoresponder. Read more about this in Chapter 10.

4. Content. Once you've set up everything above, take a look at your blog, podcast or videos. Do you create content? How often? What format is the best for you and your audience? Create an editorial calendar and get on a schedule. Read more about this in Chapter 8.

5. Promotion. Finally, let's look at your promotional activities. What have you tried that has worked in the past? Where does your ideal client hang out online? Which social media platforms do you (and your ideal client) like the best? Read more about this in Chapter 9.

If you're just getting started, you can begin with just an email list, free gift, and landing page. I've met online entrepreneurs who made their first $100,000 this way, no website required!

If you're already doing online marketing, start at the top and work through the list in order of priority. For each step, look at any data you have about how this step is currently working for you. It's often obvious where the system is getting stuck or where you can apply more focus or resources to increase results.

 A Warning about Websites: Building a website isn't included in my priority list to set up your online marketing. While a website is an important part of an online business, it's a major project that can result in lots of procrastination and perfectionism, and you simply don't need it to get started. You can create an email list, and use a basic landing page where people can subscribe (see the Book Bonuses for my latest recommendations on landing pages). With just an email list and landing page you can build your audience and make your first sales — which can ultimately fund your new website down the road.

Reality Check: What If I Need Revenue Immediately?

If you're in a situation where you need to bring in money quickly, but you're just getting started with online marketing, I want you to step away from your computer, and go meet people!

Online marketing will bring clients and revenue to your business, but it's not an instant or overnight solution. If you already have an email list and an audience online, then by all means, send them a special offer to generate revenue today. But if you're just getting started online and need money quickly, the fastest way to find customers is to meet people out in the real world. Go to a networking event. Ask for a referral. Chat up people in line at the grocery store.

And don't worry about going offline to grow online. Just because you use traditional, in-person methods to find clients doesn't mean that you've 'failed' at online business, or that it's not going to work for you. Allow clients to flow to you however it happens.

Staying Organized

If you want to spend more time doing the work you love (your actual wellness work) instead of marketing, it's essential to stay organized.

Create a single location for all of your marketing ideas, plans and notes. This can be physical or digital depending on how you like to work.

You can go further than this if you want, and put everything about your business into an online notebook. At the time of writing this, I'm doing this using Evernote, and I'll keep the Book Bonuses updated with my current recommendations.

In my digital notebook, I have notes for:

- Master to-do list (this is long!) that has everything I want or need to do, both personally and in my business

- Editorial calendar for content (see Chapter 8)

- Promotional plan (see Chapter 9)

- Annual plan for my business (I map out revenue goals and big monthly events or actions)

Because everything is in one place, and is easily searchable, nothing ever gets lost.

Before I moved to this system, I had little pieces of paper everywhere! I used about four different notebooks depending on what I had handy, plus a bunch of scraps of paper, sticky notes, anything I could write on! THAT system was stressful. I spent ages looking for ideas, notes or plans, and never felt confident that I'd remember a great idea.

Since moving to a single digital notebook, I'm totally confident that everything is captured and easily accessible.

Do I still use physical notebooks? Yes, definitely for daily planning or sketching. But at the end of the day or week, I transfer everything important into my digital notebook.

As a personal practice, I love having one single to-do list. The secret is that I never work directly from this list! (If I work from this list, then I fall into procrastination by doing the 'easiest' tasks first, rather than the most important tasks!)

Every morning, as part of my morning routine, I refocus on my major current goal, and pick three tasks from the list that will move me forward the most that day. I write down those tasks on a piece of paper, and that's the short daily to-do list I work from. Three items. Some days those three items take the entire day, and some days they're done within an hour, which lets me move on to other tasks. If I get through those three most important tasks, then I've made real progress on my business, instead of just being busy.

Over time, when I review my to-do list, some tasks fall off because they're just not important anymore. But spending some time each day prioritizing tasks that will make the biggest difference to my business (never "change the header on my Facebook page!") — then I know I'm moving forward.

There are so many different personal productivity and organization systems, you'll just need to experiment to find what works for you.

But the overall idea is to put all of your marketing and business information in a central location so you can easily find it without duplicating effort.

You'll find more information around tools and resources for being organized and productive in the Book Bonuses.

Work Efficiently by Batching

We first talked about batching in the content chapter. You can batch tasks in all areas of your business (and the rest of your life). Every time you switch tasks, it takes extra time to shift your mind into the new task and become productive and efficient at it. So why not bundle together similar tasks so you can complete them all at once? Not only is this faster and easier, but it also gets you planning ahead (instead of doing one blog post, you might write two or three), and naturally creates a process for each task, making it easier to outsource in the future.

Batching even just two or three tasks will save you lots of time.

Here are some ideas for tasks you can batch:

- Creating content
- Setting up content on your website
- Writing and uploading emails
- Creating social media updates
- Scheduling social media updates
- Creating graphics for your blog posts or website
- Creating materials for your program or workshop
- Engaging on social media (can you set a timer and engage for 15 minutes every day, rather than popping in and out of Facebook throughout the day?)
- Pitching yourself to be on podcasts or to write guest posts

- Writing your autoresponder

- Doing your accounting or bookkeeping, creating invoices, paying bills

Although it sometimes feels overly structured to batch all of your tasks for yourself, you'll quickly start to identify the repeatable tasks that could be outsourced to an assistant, which brings us to...

Recurring vs. One-Time Tasks

When you're looking at the tasks in your business, think about recurring versus one time tasks.

As the name implies, recurring tasks happen over and over again in your business. These are tasks like creating content, publishing content, posting on social media, promoting your content etc.

One time tasks happen — you guessed it! — one time. These are tasks like creating your email opt-in gift, creating an autoresponder, writing a book, writing a program or talk etc.

Make a list of the recurring tasks in your business. This will change over time as your business develops.

You'll want to schedule time in your calendar (or your assistant's calendar) each week to complete these recurring tasks. You should never be surprised or scrambling to publish a blog post, because you can see it coming weeks in advance. Schedule time each week for your recurring tasks, so you know they'll get done.

One time tasks vary every week. I like to block out regular hours to work on these types of projects. Although the actual tasks will vary each week depending on what you're working on, you know you'll have uninterrupted time to work on these strategic projects in your business.

Don't Do It All Yourself

Even if you're just starting out, start thinking about getting help in your business. There are very affordable ways to hire Virtual Assistants to help with your online marketing.

Of course as the CEO of your business, you're in charge of the online strategy. But the implementation of the strategy doesn't have to be done by you alone!

Start by identifying those recurring tasks which you don't need to do personally. For example, you might want to write your blog posts, but you don't personally need to be the one loading them into your website, or sharing them on social media.

Maybe you want to write all the materials for your new program, but you don't personally need to be the one making the professional looking PDFs, or uploading them into a course website. What about setting up your autoresponder? You can write the content for the emails, but the actual setup could be done by someone else.

Even if you choose to do all of the tasks yourself for now, start thinking in terms of tasks that only you can do compared to tasks you could train someone else to do.

Hiring a virtual assistant is beyond the scope of this book, but see the Book Bonuses for recommendations on where and how to hire Virtual Assistants.

Emergency Overwhelm Formula

It happens to the best of us: sometimes we feel overwhelmed, with too much to do, and no idea where to focus!

Here's what to do in that situation:

- Get a clean sheet of paper and move to a new location (away from your computer!)

- Do a total brain dump — make a list of everything swirling in your head, all the to-dos and actions and plans. Keep going until you get it all out. This might be a long list.

- Now put the paper aside, and for at least 10 minutes do something completely different that gets you into fresh air, sunshine or at least in touch with your body! Walk outside, stretch in the sun or do a little yoga or a workout. Have a drink of water and do not check your phone!

- After at least 10 minutes, go back inside, and reconnect with your vision from Chapter 1. This is why we keep the vision board handy (usually pinned beside my computer, or as my computer desktop background). Forget the "how" for now, and focus on the "why". Why are you doing this work? What's the change you're trying to make in the world?

- Now finally, return to your brain dump paper and review it. Are there clear priorities that jump out at you? Which are most aligned with your big goals? Which are going to move you forward the most?

This process gets it all out of your head, changes your state, refocuses you on your big vision, and soon your priorities become clear. Give it a try next time you're feeling stuck or swamped.

Support and Accountability

Just because you're running your own business doesn't mean you need to work alone.

It's really valuable to find a peer group or community to support you in your work.

You might find other wellness practitioners, or complementary business owners who could also serve as a referral network. Or other online entrepreneurs who can support you around the online marketing side of your business. Or a coach to work with you 1:1 building up your business.

You might like a small accountability or mastermind group with weekly meetings, or joining a larger less formal group for monthly meet ups. It's up to you and your work style. But just know that you don't need to build your business alone, and you don't need to reinvent the wheel. No matter if you're just getting started, or if you have an established business, you have something to learn and something to teach. Reach out. The support is there if you're open to it!

And if you can't find a group in your local area, you can either start one, or join an online group.

You can start right here within the Wellpreneur community. I'll link to our group from the Book Bonuses.

ACTION STEPS:

- Get organized! Choose one central location where you'll keep all of your marketing and business ideas and plans, and start using it.

- Make a list of the recurring and one-time tasks you need to do, and schedule them into your calendar.

- Get support! Decide what kind of support you'd like for growing your business — small group, large group, 1:1, in-person or online? Research a few options.

Amanda Cook

Wellpreneur Interview: Leonie Dawson

Leonie Dawson is an author, retreat leader, and visual artist, mama and business mentor for heart-centered, creative women. In this interview, Leonie shares how goal-setting and commitment helped her transition from government employee to million-dollar business owner. Learn more about Leonie at LeonieDawson.com.

I started my business on the side of my day job, and quickly realized I had no clue how to make enough money to do it full time. So I gave myself a year. I decided that in the next year, I'd earn $30,000 through my business doing things I love. I was determined to make it happen.

I easily could have told myself that it was too hard, that I didn't know what to do, and that I should just settle for my office job for the rest of my life. But instead, I realized that if other people had already done it, then they must know something that I don't know! No baby comes out of the womb knowing how to run a successful business or knowing how to market themselves! It's all learnable information. So, I committed to making my business work.

I created a lot of discipline around that goal. I invested in education, and whatever I learned, I implemented. I made it a habit to install whatever I learned into my business right away, rather than just adding it to my to-do list.

The results from this were profound. I did earn $30,000 that first year, and I quit my government job two years after that.

My husband always insists I remind people that I was not an overnight success. I've been working on this for 12 years.

I used to come home from my full-time job and stay up until midnight tinkering with my blog, and it wasn't making any money! And I didn't care, I just loved it. I just wanted to create, share and help people, and I showed up every single day to do that.

That mentality built up over 12 years has really had a snowball effect. The entire time, I've followed the same formula of committing to a goal, and then learning whatever I need to learn to reach it. My business has doubled or tripled in size every year.

We've just completed a $2 million year, which is beyond my wildest dreams.

Only a few years ago, I didn't even know how to make $30,000 per year, and now I feel like I could sneeze and make $30,000. It's been a really amazing journey, but the principles stay the same. Make the decision, commit, implement and have faith.

Listen to the complete interview in the Book Bonuses:
WellpreneurBook.com/bonus

Wellpreneur Interview: Latham Thomas

Latham Thomas is a celebrity wellness and lifestyle maven and birth doula. In this interview she shares how she started her business and why having a support system is so important. Learn more at MamaGlow.com.

When I was pregnant with my son in 2003, I wanted to learn everything about maternal wellness. I was the first of my friends to have a baby, so I didn't really have models to show me the way. I had assumed in New York City it would be easy to find all of this information, but I struggled to find a practitioner, get appointments, and to know which products and services were suitable for pregnancy.

Mama Glow developed really organically. It wasn't something that I set out to do, and I didn't know the shape it would take, but I knew that I was meant to help mothers and women transition into this phase of their life beautifully, and smoothly and feel supported.

I started meeting with women in my living room about maintaining optimal wellness during pregnancy. I would just lecture, or chat and answer questions. I got certified as a health coach, a yoga teacher and then finally as a doula. That really brought my business full circle. Then I started writing my book, and that's when it really took off.

When you feel called to go somewhere, but you don't know why, just go. That's where you find connections, ideas, and the people who will be your biggest supporters. There's always a reason you feel called to do something. It's not up to you to debate with your soul and psych yourself out. It's your job to listen. That's the biggest lesson we can learn as entrepreneurs. When we're listening, the soul can speak to us, and let us know exactly what our next step is. I think the reason many entrepreneurs feel so uncertain about where to go next is because they've stopped listening.

When my son was small, I would hustle in the time he was sleeping. I would bring him with me to everything I did. If he couldn't come, I wouldn't do the job. It was very clear my priority was to be with him. But in those hours when he was in nursery school three hours a day, three days a week, I would work.

You really need a supportive community to help you through. You know the saying "It takes a village to raise a child?" Well, it takes a village to launch a business too.

I suggest finding a sister circle (which can include brothers too.) It's people who cheer for you, who believe in you, who support you and who see your blind spots. Find people who will support where you're headed, not just where you are right now.

Listen to the complete interview in the Book Bonuses:
WellpreneurBook.com/bonus

Conclusion

"Begin doing what you want to do now. We are not living in eternity. We have only this moment, sparkling like a star in our hand and melting like a snowflake."

— Francis Bacon

Before I started this business, I was living in London and had a lengthy commute into my corporate job. I'd bring my laptop or my notebook for the 90-minute journey and furiously write blog posts for my natural beauty blog. I remember feeling intensely driven to *just make this work*, and equally frustrated that it wasn't happening faster. I remember two mornings in particular when I just cried on the way to work, feeling so angry and resentful about having to "waste my time" going to an office job.

Fast forward to early 2016, when my husband had the opportunity to move to Hong Kong for his job.

We didn't think twice about it, we just immediately accepted. By that time, I was working fully for myself, on my own business, and because I work with my clients online, I can work from anywhere in the world. Aside from some early morning calls because of the timezone change, being in London or Hong Kong didn't make a difference to my business.

But it made a huge difference to me personally.

Amanda Cook

Sitting at my desk, looking at the Hong Kong skyline, I feel so grateful that I stuck with my online business through the early ups and downs and frustrations, so that I have the flexibility to be here in Asia, and travel whenever I want. I don't know what we would have done if I'd still been in my corporate job. It would have been a much more difficult decision to move, if we'd done it at all.

I hope this book has helped you to see the reality — good and bad — of growing your wellness business online.

Is online marketing your ticket to an immediate overnight success? Probably not. But if you want to build a business that fits your life, gives you both location and time freedom, and lets you impact thousands of people around the world — I truly believe growing your business online is the way to go.

My initial vision of creating my business online was to give me time and location independence. But I hadn't anticipated all the amazing real-world connections that I'd make in the process. I've met wellpreneurs and other inspiring, soulful, online entrepreneurs around the world. We've spent time together — in person — in London and Bangkok and the Philippines and Hong Kong. I hear from readers and listeners in Australia, and Kenya, and South Carolina and Lithuania. The farther I go on this online business journey, the more I realize how small the world is, how we're all connected, and what a big difference one motivated person can make.

You CAN create your wellness business online. You just need a vision, a community for support, and most importantly — the willingness and tenacity to stick with it!

This is the best time to be a health and wellness entrepreneur. The world clearly needs our help, and people everywhere are waking up to the fact that they can improve their wellbeing — they just need to know how. It's the right time to bring more wellbeing online. Will you join us?

Join Us To Grow Your Wellness Business!

Subscribe to The Wellpreneur Podcast
Over 100,000 Downloads and 70 5-Star Reviews in iTunes!

The Wellpreneur Podcast is a weekly show about marketing and business for wellness entrepreneurs. Join Amanda Cook as she interviews the most successful, inspiring wellness entrepreneurs about their tips, advice and lessons learned for growing a wellness business online. Learn more at: WellpreneurOnline.com

"I'm completely hooked on this podcast! High quality with so much essential information!"
— luckyleaf

"Amanda's podcast lights a fire under you to work on your business goals!"
— Kate L.

"This podcast is SO needed in the crowded space of people trying to make money online."

— ProBalanceTV

"Just finished listening to ALL of the podcasts, then went back and listened again to take notes! A must listen for any wellness pro!"

— Rick G

"I love this podcast! It's exactly what I've been looking for. I've learned so much, and can't stop listening. Amanda teaches the things you don't learn about starting a business in school!"

— Maggie M

"I love listening and can't get enough! The guests provide tons of value and actionable tips. I have to keep my notebook next to me because it sparks so many ideas."

— Claudia P.

"These podcasts are an incredible resource. So much insight, inspiration and Amanda has a knack for bringing things down to a practical level. So so useful!"

— Laura J.

"Amanda Cook is a craftswoman of podcasts!!"

— Czarina

"I listen to your podcasts in the car all.the.time. So much that my daughter renamed her American Girl doll Amanda Cook! :)"

— lmhaley33

Join Us for Marketing Bootcamp

The proven step-by-step program to bring more of the right people to your website, and turn them into paying clients, so you can spend more time doing the work you love!
Learn more at: WellpreneurOnline.com/bootcamp

"During the program, I created a guest blog post based on your system, and got over 111 subscribers in the first seven hours! Since taking Bootcamp, my list has grown over 85%, I have a clear system to show me why each step is important, and a focus on creating content that my audience wants instead of obsessing over open rates. If you want to learn how to create a sales funnel that will help you reach your business goals — join Bootcamp!"

— EJ Ogenyi, Team by EJ Ogenyi.

"Marketing Bootcamp helped me figure out my niche — that's huge! It gave me focus, clarity and helped me feel "unstuck". My email list has also grown over 20% during the program, and now I have a plan and know

what to do to continue growing. Bootcamp provided in-depth, practical, actionable advice and the focus specifically for wellpreneurs made it even more valuable."

— Naomi Nakamura, Live FAB Life

"Since Bootcamp, I've had so many people interested in my work, I signed on one new client and have two others who are really interested! Bootcamp is approachable and totally actionable, and for me, really has produced results — both online and off. Thank you for the confidence and guidance you've given me. It came at just the right time, and has made me realize that this dream of mine really is possible!"

— Samantha Russell, Live the Whole

"I was worried that I was always spending too much money on courses without finding that "thing" that would really make a difference. But since applying what I learned in Marketing Bootcamp, starting with creating a fabulous opt-in for my list with three videos — I signed my first client from my new email sequence! I have also sold my first online course from the same email sequence. Now I'm getting so much more interaction with my email subscribers, they email me back all the time which I love! I recommend the program to anyone who wants an online health coaching business — I mean anyone! It's easy. It helps you run your business more effectively. It helps you take action. And it works! :)"

— Emma Polette, Blue Sky Vitality

Acknowledgements

Publishing this book was a huge team effort, and after two years of talking about it, I'm so thankful for the support and encouragement to finally make it a reality!

A big thank you to…

My husband Zak, for providing feedback and a listening ear to my obsession with digital marketing and book covers these past few months.

My assistant Marija, who kept everything running smoothly in the business so I could focus on the book, and helped with innumerable details in actually getting the book out the door!

Laura Hanly, for your keen editor's eye and smart advice during the final weeks of bringing the book into the world!

Nichole, for encouraging me to write this book when it was just a wisp of an idea.

My mastermind buddies, who are the ultimate supportive sounding board and constantly expand my vision for what's possible.

The Wellpreneur Book Ambassador Team, for your feedback, support, encouragement, enthusiasm and sharing throughout the book creation process!

Amanda Cook

The Wellpreneur Community, who inspire me everyday to continue doing this work, as I watch your success in spreading wellness around the world!

And, of course, my parents, who have always supported my choices, even when I take the non-traditional path!

About the Author

Amanda Cook is a digital marketer, award winning health coach, and host of The Wellpreneur Podcast, one of the top business podcasts on iTunes, reaching over 10,000 wellness entrepreneurs each month. She has interviewed more than 112 successful wellness entrepreneurs about how they built healthy businesses online, and has spoken at events on five continents. Her work has appeared in *The Huffington Post UK*, *The Sunday Telegraph*, *Natural Health Magazine*, *MindBodyGreen*, *TinyBuddha* and *Copyblogger*. Amanda teaches wellness entrepreneurs around the world to grow their business through digital marketing in her Wellpreneur Marketing Bootcamp, and lives in London and Hong Kong. Learn more at WellpreneurOnline.com.

Made in the USA
Columbia, SC
26 August 2018